ISSUES IN MISSIOLOGY
AN INTRODUCTION

ISSUES IN MISSIOLOGY
AN INTRODUCTION

EDWARD C. PENTECOST

BAKER BOOK HOUSE
Grand Rapids, Michigan 49506

To
my dear wife and colaborer
who has been my constant help
and companion

Contents

Foreword

Missiology is a science that has only recently been recognized as a valid concept in its own right. It is the product of years of development and recognizes the contribution that the humanities can make to the understanding and execution of the missionary task.

Until rather recent times the work of missions was seen to be solely the work of the Holy Spirit, guiding and empowering men as His instruments of outreach which proclaim the divine message of redemption to the lost. Previously there was little recognition of the necessity or legitimacy of input from human sciences.

William Carey fought a battle against the institution which held so strongly to the doctrine of the sovereignty of God and His absolute control that it refused to recognize the legitimate use of means to accomplish a purpose. Yet Carey launched out with the formation of a mission board, and the modern era of missions was born. In no way does the movement minimize the work or control of the sovereignty of God. It only recognizes the mission board as an instrument in the hands of God to accomplish His sovereign purpose.

Missionaries have gone out in response to the call, totally committed to God and to the lost. Their total surrender has not only been recognized but fully appreciated. Nothing will ever become a substitute for that. However, the experiences of many men and women who have given their lives to serve have aroused questions. Many have asked others, "How have *you* done the work?" There has developed a sharing of experiences between missionaries themselves and their mission boards. Methodology has been compared and case studies developed. Anthropology has become a significant element in missions studies, and anthropologists have made a very significant contribution, as missionaries have begun to look for better understanding of target peoples. Missionaries have come to understand that though the message is absolute and unchangeable, yet the differences between peoples make an understanding of the message more a sociological matter. Communication of the message becomes clearer as communication principles are more widely implemented. Likewise, the science of psychology contributes to the communication process as the diversity of mentalities is better comprehended.

Missiology is, therefore, a science that is becoming recognized as a science, drawing from the fields of anthropology, sociology, psychology, and communications, as well as from the experience of those who have pioneered various mission endeavors. Missiology is seen today as a vital field of study in its own right. Although it does not pretend to have all the answers, missiology is becoming a valuable tool in the hands of Spirit-led men and women who are committed to a task, assisting them in the accomplishment of that goal to which they have given themselves.

The science is not easy; nor is it of human understanding alone. It is a composite of understanding that emerges from carefully selected information derived from all the humanities, conscientiously weighed in the balance of Biblical truth.

The purpose of this book is to show the multiplicity of disciplines which contribute to the field of missiology, and to recommend that the various subjects introduced be studied in greater depth. Missiology will never replace, or in any way diminish, the work of the Holy Spirit in missions. It is only hoped that the understanding gained will enhance the servant of the Lord in his comprehension of the nature and magnitude of the task, of the best possible means of undertaking the work, and of his part or place in the process. The understanding should add to his dependence upon the Lord to give the harvest, while doing all within his power to be the best equipped person for the use of the Lord Himself.

Edward C. Pentecost

1

Missionary Theology

A theology of missions starts with God, and asks the question, "What has God revealed concerning Himself and His plan for man?" It presupposes God and accepts Scripture as God's accurate, progressive, and sufficient revelation of Himself to man. This theology recognizes that God's absolute is limited by man's language, culture, context, comprehension, and finite limitations, and is interpreted within that framework.

A missions theology includes a study of the revelation of God concerning the origin of missions, the aim of missions, the plan of missions, and the consummation of missions.

As stated, all theology begins with God. Although man may systematize, organize, and formulate the expression, ultimately this is only man's imperfect understanding of the self-revelation of God, perceived within man's own context and limited understanding. The limiting factor is man's inability to comprehend the unfathomable. The absolute is God and His self-revelation given in Scripture and in the person of Jesus Christ. The limitation is man's comprehension in human language, culture, and context.

Although "The heavens are telling of the glory of God; and their expanse is declaring the work of His hands" (Ps. 19:1), yet only by indirect revelation do they reveal God. This revelation is worthy of consideration and contemplation, but limited in scope and precision.

There are those who make the study of missiology an entity

in which theology is seen as one segment equal in value to the study of the social sciences. In this system missiology is studied as a subject comprehending various disciplines of equal value, as demonstrated in Figure 1.

There are others who would subject theology to the rule of culture, making culture normative. This position declares that what culture considers right is right for that culture. The conclusion is that there is no absolute for right or wrong, but the position fails to recognize the depravity of man. It recognizes that sin is present in every culture, but the definition of sin varies from culture to culture. Therefore some act may be sinful in one culture, but not so in another. The criterion for judg-

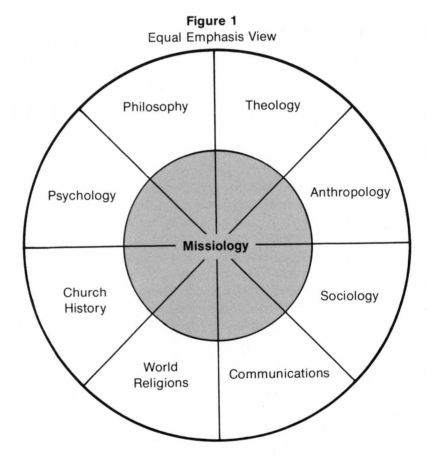

Figure 1
Equal Emphasis View

ment is the culture itself. Thus culture becomes absolute and normative. This presents a most subtle danger.

In the light of the fact that all academic disciplines are colored by one's theology, or one's concept of God and His sovereignty over all, it is the firm position taken here that theology is not a discipline to be considered on an equal basis with the social sciences, nor is theology subject to culture. All study of the social sciences is to be undertaken subject to the scrutiny and authority of a Biblical theology. Thus theology is removed from a position of equality with the social sciences, and the social sciences are placed in a subservient position, subject to theology and the scrutiny of Scripture. See Figure 2.

Figure 2
Theological Perspective View

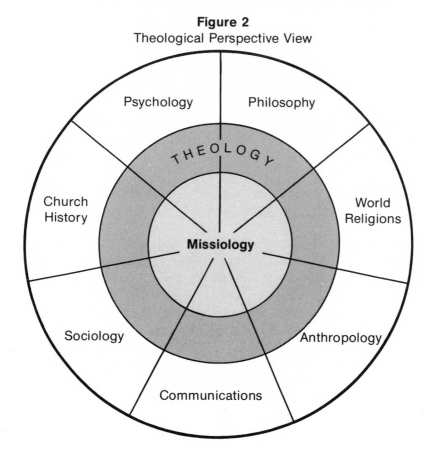

In this perspective the social sciences do not define man; rather, theology defines man in his nature and character. Sociology may declare how man operates under given conditions, but theology declares what he is. Man cannot define sin. God has defined it. How can man with a sinful nature define sin when he is subject to it?

Likewise, a theistic evolutionary position which denies the literalness of Adam and Eve and the fall of man very clearly influences one's comprehension of the origin and nature of man, as does a literal creationist position which accepts direct creation and the fall of man as literal and real. One's understanding of the character and nature of man is affected. One's understanding of sin is affected. One's relationship with God is affected. Therefore one's understanding of man's social actions and responses is also affected.

The position accepted by this author is that Scripture is literal; that man was created because God acted; and that man sinned because he was deceived. Sin brought a literal fall and condemnation. Man, therefore, has a sin nature, and is deprived of his original innocence. Man is in need of redemption; God acted on behalf of man to provide redemption. That is the same truth revealed to all men of all times in all the world.

The Origin of Missions

Although Genesis 3:15 has historically been considered as the first promise of a Redeemer, its significance can only be understood in the light of New Testament fulfillment. Ephesians 1 gives the real origin of redemption being in God before the foundation of the world. Thus we understand that God did not conceive of a plan to redeem man after man sinned, but purposed even before He created man to provide the Redeemer. God, by His very nature, is a loving and redeeming God. Missions has its origin in the very nature of God Himself.

Missions is the action of an everloving Being. It is expressed succinctly in John 3:16 and reiterated in 1 Peter 1:20, 21, "For He was foreknown before the foundation of the world, but has appeared in these last times for the sake of you who through Him are believers in God. . . ."

Such a position demands the recognition of a singular, monotheistic Being. God is One, and there is no other. Such is the message of the Old Testament, "Hear, O Israel! The LORD is our God, the Lord is one!" (Deut. 6:4). Therefore He alone is Absolute, Sovereign, Lord, King, Maker of heaven and earth.

From Him all creation had its origin and by Him all things exist. By nature, then, all is subject to Him. Throughout Scripture, all forms of idolatry are denounced and forbidden. All idolatry is sin, because it is opposed to the very nature of the one God and Creator. Out of monotheism and divine sovereignty emanates, by the very nature of the being of God, a missionary essence and message to bring *all* under the sovereign control of the one Creator. All people are of necessity connected with the one God because there is none other.

The Bible declares how separation from subservience to the one and only God happened. The first man passed the same sin nature to all men. Sin came in disobedience to the Sovereign, and is the same in nature for all mankind. But when sin came, it met a plan of redemption for all sinners, a plan that was already prepared. The plan is the same for all mankind regardless of culture, custom, context, or mentality. Man is in the same spiritual condition the world over. The same plan of redemption is effective *for* all and offered *to* all equally.

The Aim of Missions

"For as in Adam all die, so also in Christ all shall be made alive" (1 Cor. 15:22) expresses God's statement concerning His divine intention. God purposed in Christ to provide a way by which all men might be redeemed.

Initiated as the act of God and carried out as the program of God, missions has one aim: ". . . to seek and to save that which was lost" (Luke 19:10). In this, all missionaries are "fellow workers" together with God (1 Cor. 3:9). To them is committed the ministry of reconciliation (2 Cor. 5:18).

In the study of Scripture we often focus on Christ as the central figure to whom all Scripture points, and rightly so. Christ is the One revealed in Scripture. But another focus must not be lost: God's concern for man. God's concern for man caused Him to send His Son into the world as Redeemer. In this we see man as the end or focus, and Christ as the means. God's purpose was to restore man to the position intended for him and in which man is presented as without sin in Revelation 21 and 22. Christ is the means by which redemption and restoration come to man. See Figure 3.

In writing to Timothy, Paul expresses the very heart of Christian missions. He shows how God, who is both creator and sovereign, has made it known that "[He] desires all men to be saved and to come to the knowledge of the truth" (1 Tim. 2:4). The motivation is the infinite love of the sovereign God. As creator He loves His creatures. As sovereign He determines to provide, in love, a way by which fallen man can return to Himself.

Isaiah stated it, "Turn to Me, and be saved, all the ends of the earth; For I am God, and there is no other" (Isa. 45:22).

In order for the aim of God to be fulfilled, the program of God must be completed. The message must be announced to all mankind in all the world. God's aim is to provide eternal

Figure 3
The Span of Missions

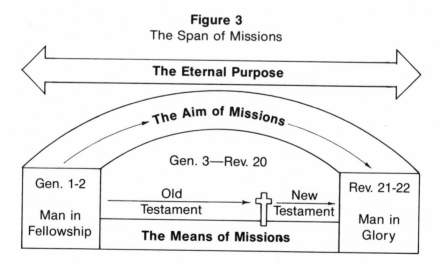

life. Jesus Christ brought it. Now the ministry of reconciliation is committed to men (2 Cor. 5:18). Men are the message bearers.

The Plan of Missions

God's program for the ages is clearly a plan of divine origin. It was conceived by God before the foundation of the world, progressively revealed to man through the ages of world history, brought to man through the death and resurrection of Christ, and finally to be carried to culmination in the fulfillment of the eternal kingdom of God.

In outline form we may illustrate the program of God as shown in Figure 4.

God's program has one constant element: God has never left Himself without a witness to draw men to Himself (Acts 14:17). Before sin entered into the heart of man, God entered in the cool of the evening to converse with Adam. Adam had personal communion with his Creator and enjoyed the divine presence in a most real way. Sin entered and destroyed that fellowship. Yet Adam still had the memory of those blessed days. From father to son the memory was transmitted. Sin, however, soon took over, and man became violent and wicked in every imagination of his heart. See Genesis 6.

In the midst of such declared opposition, God chose a man to be His witness to the new generation. For the first time, God became selective on behalf of all mankind. God was, in method, a particularist, choosing Noah to be a universal witness. To Noah was given a blueprint of a plan of redemption from the flood which would come upon all humanity. For 100 years Noah was in the process of building the ark. During that time he was a living witness to all of his generation. Peter proclaims him to be "a preacher of righteousness" (2 Peter 2:5). Noah's secret was that he believed God. His belief worked his salvation. His redemption was particular. The offer was universal. The pattern and example were given and visible. Any other individual could have built himself an ark, or could have entered with Noah into his ark before the door was shut. The opportunity was available. Disbelief stood between the

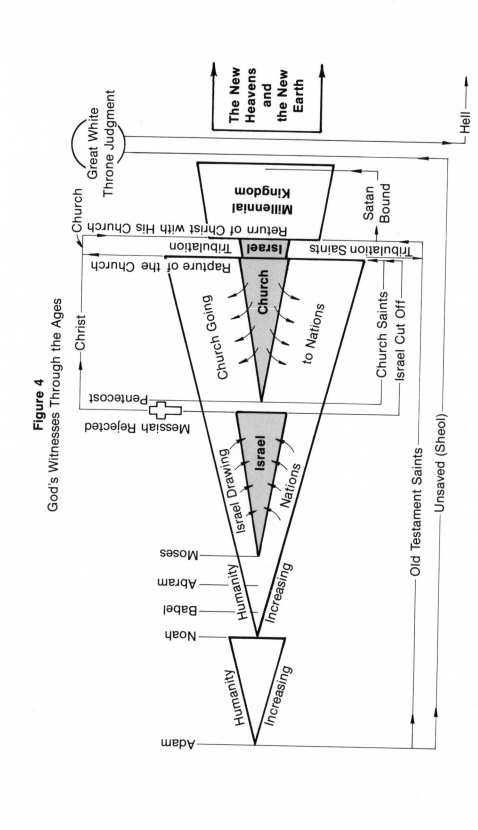

Figure 4
God's Witnesses Through the Ages

individual and salvation. God provided a universal pattern for redemption through a particular individual.

With the sons of Noah the same pattern of communication of father to son prevailed, as had prevailed from Adam to Noah. Man's response was essentially the same in the generations following Noah until, at Babel, God confounded the languages and divided men into linguistic groups. From this dispersion nations emerged according to language and geographic boundaries. Languages became diversified, and cultures grew distinct; yet man's nature remained the same universally.

Then came the call of God again to one particular individual, Abram, to whom a promise was given on behalf of all nations, ". . . in you all the families of the earth shall be blessed" (Gen. 12:3). God's particular choice was on behalf of all mankind. His method was to choose one through whom He would bless many.

Following Abraham God again moved to another, Moses. Through Moses God called a nation to be His chosen nation on behalf of all nations. God committed to Moses the message for all the nation of Israel, saying, "Now then, if you will indeed obey My voice and keep My covenant, then you shall be My own possession among all the peoples, for all the earth is Mine; and you shall be to Me a kingdom of priests and a holy nation" (Exod. 19:5,6).

One particular nation was chosen to be that nation that would stand as priest before God on behalf of the other nations. Israel was to be intercessor between God and the nations of the world. God's action was with a universal purpose to all mankind, working through Israel as His particularly chosen vehicle of communication. Israel was to be that nation over whom the cloud and the pillar of fire remained. Jehovah was the name of the Almighty God of Israel, maker of heaven and earth. All the idolatrous nations were to see and recognize the difference in Israel, and be drawn to Israel's God. Israel's position was a choice position, but one of great responsibility. Through Israel God would reveal Himself to all the nations of the world.

Israel, in her very formation as a nation in Egypt, was a witness to the Egyptians. The real conflict presented was between Jehovah and the gods of Pharaoh and Egypt. The commandments given to Moses in the Book of Exodus were commandments given to separate Jehovah's people as a peculiar people unto Himself and for His purpose. Within this body were Israelites who were born Israelites, and those who were drawn to Israel to become followers of Jehovah. Thus Moses was commanded: "The same law shall apply to the native as to the stranger who sojourns among you" (Exod. 12:49; Lev. 24:22; Num. 15:14-16). This applied even to celebrating the Passover, the most holy feast of Israel.

The tabernacle was a special display of the presence of Jehovah, the almighty God, with His people before all the nations to see. The wilderness wanderings were seen and known by all the surrounding nations. When Israel finally came to Canaan, the word concerning the defeat of Pharaoh had preceded their arrival, and fear was in the heart of all the people of Jericho (Josh. 2:9-11). Thus Jericho was defeated before the people of Israel even arrived.

Turning to the Psalter we find expressed most clearly the ultimate desire of Jehovah for all the world. Practically, the Psalms served to unite Israel in praise and worship. They were a collection of hymns to be used in sanctuary worship. As prayers and hymns of praise they were devotional. Theologically, however, they declare God's nature, attributes, perfections, works of creation, sovereignty, providence, and grace. They declare His supremacy over all principalities, and celebrate His control over all the nations and universe.

Israel may have seen the Psalms from a particularist view, yet a universal application and appeal is unmistakable. Notice Psalms 2, 33, 66, 67, 96, 98, 100, 117, 145, to mention a few.

Passing from the Old Testament perspective of God's providing a particular witness before all nations to draw the nations to Himself, in the New Testament we see Christ offered as the one and only substitute for all men. He was God's Redeemer provided for mankind. Redemption was accomplished through Him.

A unique Redeemer was necessary as a mediator between God and man. He was needed because of the breach that sin had caused between the two. "For as in Adam all die, so also in Christ all shall be made alive" (1 Cor. 15:22). Thus comes the fulfillment of the provision of the sovereign Creator, in the person of His own Son, who is uniquely God-man, through the program eternally designed to make redemption possible for all men.

G. Christian Weiss in *The Heart of Missionary Theology* expresses it:

> The wonder of God's grace and the Gospel is that, before man was ever created, Jesus Christ was ordained to become the great mediator—the go-between, the advocate, the reconciler, the peacemaker—between a holy, righteous God and sinful, depraved man.[1]

God's program rested upon the uniqueness of Christ, the only Savior for mankind who was both God and man, thus able to fill both divine and human demands.

Paul becomes the New Testament theologian regarding God's plan. Romans is his most prolific treatise explaining God's program and provision. In it he starts with God in His sovereignty, and shows God as the Initiator, who by His nature moved on behalf of men. Not only was salvation offered to the Jews but to the Gentiles. Thus, through the one chosen nation, and the one chosen Redeemer, salvation was offered to all men of all nations.

Then the Holy Spirit was given in God's order to "seal" the redeemed (2 Cor. 1:21,22; 2 Cor. 5:5; Eph. 1:13,14).

In this present age the particular body through which God moves to provide His blessing to all mankind is the Church, entrusted with the message of reconciliation and commanded to "go" and to "preach" to all nations (Matt. 28:19,20; Mark 16:15).

The missionary message is a message that is now unmis-

---

1. G. Christian Weiss, *The Heart of Missionary Theology*. (Chicago: Moody Press, 1977), p. 33.

takable. God's progressive revelation has come to its ultimate, and did so in the words of Christ Himself when He said, "Go therefore and make disciples of all the nations . . ." accompanied by His promise: ". . . and lo, I am with you always, even to the end of the age" (Matt. 28:19,20).

As theologian, Paul presents God's program of missions by first presenting God as the sovereign from whom missions flow and the author of missions. (Eph. 1:3-14; Eph. 3:1-11; 2 Cor. 5:18; 2 Tim. 1:8-10; Rom. 16:25-27). He then portrays Christ as the Redeemer for all mankind, being sent from God to be Savior and Lord, the exclusive One (Rom. 8:3,4; Gal. 4:4).

Paul's theology carries him to the message of the gospel, and to the church as the agent in the world today. The object and ultimate concern is that all might be saved (1 Cor. 15:1-4; 1 Cor. 3:16; 2 Cor. 6:16; Eph. 2:21,22).

The Holy Spirit is then presented, equally partner in God's plan, working in men, convincing and enlightening, causing them to believe. He too was sent from the Father and is the Controller of the church, Christ's body. He is the giver of gifts, and the executor of God's program. (Titus 3:5; Eph. 2:1-10; Rom. 8:5; Gal. 4:4,5; 2 Cor. 4:4; 1 Cor. 2:4; Eph. 2:15; Rom. 12:3-8; 1 Cor. 12:1-12; Eph. 4:11,12).

The Consummation of Missions

John is the writer called upon to reveal the concluding chapter of God's eternal plan. He writes of the great tribulation period when God again turns to His chosen nation of Israel to be His witness in the end times. The church is raptured and no longer God's witness on the earth. Her work is done. God turns again to the nation Israel for His purpose, that on the earth there shall be a witness to His name. The "times of the Gentiles" comes to its conclusion, the seventh angel sounds his trumpet, and "The kingdom of the world has become *the kingdom* of our Lord, and of His Christ; and He will reign forever and ever" (Rev. 11:15).

Revelation 21 and 22 then present the culmination, where

the redeemed are with God—His purpose and program accomplished.

Our final point concerns the uniqueness of this present period. God has in His love entrusted the privilege of being colaborers together with Him to His church. That body is given the command to preach the gospel to every creature. Some are allowed to preach, and declare by word of mouth the message of redemption. Some are called upon to be "martyrs" for the truth, who through giving their lives witness to the truth.

The message is undeniable, "[Christ] gave Himself as a ransom for all" (1 Tim. 2:6). The witness is to be carried to all creatures for whom Christ Himself is the ransom. Thus divine sovereignty and grace unite with human instrumentality in the proclamation of the message to all people and tongues and tribes and nations.

As Israel was a privileged nation with the responsibility of stewardship, so the church is entrusted with a divine appointment and solemn stewardship.

Bibliography

Anderson, Gerald H., ed. *The Theology of the Christian Mission*. New York: McGraw-Hill, 1961.

Blauw, Johannes. *The Missionary Nature of the Church: A Survey of the Biblical Theology of Missions*. New York: McGraw-Hill, 1962.

Carver, William Owen. *Missions in the Plan of the Ages*. Old Tappan, NJ: Fleming H. Revell, 1909.

Glover, Robert Hall. *The Bible Basis of Missions*. Chicago: Moody Press, 1966.

Hahn, Ferdinand. *Missions in the New Testament*. Translated by Frank Clarke. Geneva, AL: Alec R. Allenson, 1965.

Hesselgrave, David J., ed. *Theology and Mission*. Grand Rapids: Baker Book House, 1978.

Johnston, Arthur P. *World Evangelism and the Word of God*. Minneapolis: Bethany Fellowship, 1974.

Kane, J. Herbert. *Christian Missions in Biblical Perspective*. Grand Rapids: Baker Book House, 1976.

_____*Understanding Christian Missions*. Grand Rapids: Baker Book House, 1978.

Lindsell, Harold. *An Evangelical Theology of Missions*. Grand Rapids: Zondervan, 1970.

Peters, George W. *A Biblical Theology of Missions*. Chicago: Moody Press, 1972.

Power, John. *Mission Theology Today*. Maryknoll, NY: Orbis Books, 1971.

Rossel, Jacques. *Mission in a Dynamic Society*. Geneva, AL: Alec R. Allenson, 1968.

Stott, John R. W. *Christian Mission in the Modern World*. Downers Grove, IL: Inter-Varsity Press, 1976.

Taylor, John V. *The Go-between God: The Holy Spirit and the Christian Mission*. New York: Oxford University Press, 1979.

Vicedom, Georg F. *The Mission of God*. Translated by Gilbert A. Thiele and Dennis Hilgendorf. St. Louis: Concordia Publishing, 1965.

Weiss, G. Christian. *The Heart of Missionary Theology*. Chicago: Moody Press, 1977.

Wright, G. Ernest. *God Who Acts: Biblical Theology as Recital*. London: SCM Press, 1964.

2

The Scriptural Context

Scripture is so aligned with the culture of Bible times that it is often difficult to distinguish between that which is fundamental and permanent, and that which is cultural and open to change and adaptation. At the same time Scripture is so positive concerning certain practices that no one can mistake its clear-cut demands of separation.

Caesar Augustus decreed that everyone had to go to his village of birth to pay the levied tax. This mandate took Joseph and Mary to Bethlehem where the Christ was born. Obedience to the decree led to the fulfillment of prophecy. Here conformity to practice was clearly in order.

The whole pattern of Israelitic society was guided by the dictates of their religious practices. Absolute separation from the idols and idolatrous practices of the neighboring peoples was demanded. Paul taught the Romans that there was a place for nonconformity in Romans 12:2, "And do not be conformed to this world, but be transformed by the renewing of your mind, that you may prove what the will of God is, that which is good and acceptable and perfect."

Immediately a premise stands out: Separation from evil is demanded, and separation unto holiness is equally exhorted (Rom. 12:21; 1 Peter 1:15,16).

The phrase, "But when the fulness of the time came, God sent forth His Son, born under the Law, in order that He might redeem those who were under the Law, that we might receive the adoption as sons" (Gal. 4:4-5), may have more

27

cultural implications than we at first presume. God was molding a certain cultural setting around His chosen people, the nation of Israel. When Christ was born all the cultural, social, and political context was completed for the fulfillment of the prophecies which His prophets had announced beforehand. The cultural setting was not simply God adapting Himself to man's culture, but was a predetermined and controlled setting that God had engineered to bring into being at His appointed time for the fulfillment of His eternal purpose. Every aspect of every prophecy was fulfilled according to His design.

If this is true, then we find that the pattern of culture may be more important than has been previously recognized. It is vital that we understand the cultural context of Scripture if we would comprehend the message of Scripture. The religio-cultural context of the Old Testament setting, with the practice of sacrifice, is most necessary for an understanding of the message transmitted in the words, "for Christ our Passover also has been sacrificed" (1 Cor. 5:7) or John's proclamation, ". . . Behold, the Lamb of God" (John 1:36).

Also the crucifixion could only have been carried out within such a prepared context. Crucifixion was a Roman method of execution for the crime Christ was accused of. The Jews would have stoned Him. Yet prophecy declared, ". . . he who is hanged is accursed of God" (Deut. 21:23), restated by Paul, "Cursed is everyone who hangs on a tree" clearly referring to Christ (Gal. 3:13).

The study of Scripture itself demonstrates how deeply embedded the message is in the cultural setting in which it was given; so deeply embedded, in fact, that at times the message is completely missed if the context is not understood. The message cannot be extracted from the culture in which it was given, while at the same time it must be made equally relevant to the culture in which it is to be lived.

Christ came into the world to seek and to save that which was lost. That is an absolute, universal, unqualified truth. He was born in a given city, Bethlehem, and laid in a manger. That is both a historical and a contextual statement. His birth cannot be placed in any other city than Bethlehem. That is a historical and geographic place. He was laid in a feeding trough. That is a fact. To translate the statement, "He was laid in a crib" because the crib is the place where we lay babies is to do injustice to the truth. *Manger* has implications of poverty and humility that crib does not convey. The gifts of the wise men, gold, frankincense, and myrrh, had special cultural significance. The wise men brought gifts that fit God's intent, not just any gifts. That fact cannot be separated from the gifts by choosing other gifts that might be culturally recognized by a target group. Otherwise we might have medicine men bringing dried fish, camphor boughs, and coconut oil. This would not be true to either fact or intent.

There is no doubt but that God's message is relevant to each culture, and intended for people of every culture. It is not a message for first–century Christians alone. It is a message to be communicated to every man in his own culture. Thus the missionary is challenged with the responsibility to communicate an absolute truth, given in a cultural setting and pertinent to that setting, into another cultural context and to make it relevant to the individual in that setting.

The missionary must face that challenge because of the absoluteness of the message, and the fact that culture is the vehicle of religion in any society. How a truth is communicated within a culture may well determine whether it is accepted or rejected. The fact of whether it is truth or error may not be questioned or considered by the target group. Just because the scriptural message is absolute truth does not guarantee that it will be accepted by any group. Culture provides the reference point which gives direction and meaning to life. To destroy or discredit one's culture is to make communicating the gospel to him an impossible task. The presentation of the message, and how it relates to felt needs within the culture, may determine the degree of acceptance.

Within every culture there are those aspects which can serve as bridges of communication. They must be sought out. There are aspects of culture which have no special relationship to the message, and which do not affect its transmission, but other aspects are crucial, and must be carefully considered. Two phases of presentation must be kept in mind:

1. the initial communication phase
2. the adaptation phase

Paul, in his address in Athens (Acts 17:16-31), was directing his words to the first phase. He recognized the cultural and religious context and addressed himself to it, not crediting the unknown god as legitimate, but recognizing it as a bridge. However, Paul would never have used the idol to adopt that figure as the God of whom he was speaking, to set such a figure up as the true God.

Cultural norms, practices, or objects may be used as bridges, moving from the known to the unknown. Yet, when it comes to the establishment of the church, the real issue of what is permissible comes to the fore.

The history of missions has demonstrated three distinct positions of adaptation: (1) total rejection of the old, (2) total rejection of suggestion of change, and (3) a compromise position.

1. Total rejection of the old culture theologically condemned everything of the culture as being depraved. In this position everything possible to change was changed, and a list of taboos was usually formulated. Usually the missionary's culture was established as the Christian culture, and Christian norms were clearly delineated, including dress, attendance at meetings, and giving up certain practices. Often severe discipline was imposed on any who broke the rules.

This has been the position of those who demand that a polygamist must put away all but his first wife before he be accepted in the church. Fetishes, idols, or magical implements had to be destroyed, and often a period of "probation" was necessary before a new believer could be considered part of the group.

2. Total rejection of suggestion of change is the opposite extreme—the position that cultural practices are not the missionary's concern. He considered himself as a messenger to

present the message of redemption, leaving the Holy Spirit to do all the "convicting," "convincing," and "instructing" of the new believers. No guidelines were established except those which the new believers established for themselves.

3. The compromise position scrutinized a culture according to scriptural standards concerning issues to which Scripture directly addressed itself. Some of those issues were idolatry, sacrifice, cannibalism, and infanticide. Issues that were not directly addressed were carefully considered by both the missionary and the national believers, who determined guidelines concerning practices within the local culture.

In the course of such study there are certain things that emerge:

1. The Scripture is always the norm in issues to which it addresses itself directly. All cultures come under the judgment of Scripture. Therefore, there are some practices that must demand separation. Separation from idols and known evil is an absolute. Therefore, when a practice is recognized as evil it must go.

2. There are issues that, though condemned by Scripture, cannot immediately be eliminated. Such practices include polygamy, self-inflicted bodily injury, and infant mistreatment due to cultural practices. The church can effect a change in these areas, but only after years of teaching.

3. There are practices that may need to undergo change in order to become acceptable to Christian groups. Festivities dedicated to idolatrous practices may be sanctified and changed to become acceptable practices, filled with new meaning. Drama and music may be given new direction and usefulness.

4. Some practices may be accepted without outward change, only changing internal content, such as the posture or manner of prayer or worship. There is no reason that a convert from Islam could not carry his prayer mat and pray five times a day by bowing his head to the ground. If he did it to Allah before being saved could he not do it to Yahweh after being saved? But the testimony of separation unto Christ becomes a real issue if he still performs the old ritual. Some may observe that his testimony does not show the change if he carries on his

old practice. Is that worse than being accused of not praying after he turned to Jesus Christ? Here is where he needs a new form.

5. Some forms will be designed to reflect the new concepts, new thoughts, and new truths. Patterns for baptism that are scriptural will be accepted. A pattern for remembrance of the Lord's table will be initiated.

Certain factors in Christianity are universal, and thus there is a Christian culture that is transcultural. Christianity is not indigenous to any culture. It is transmissible to all. As well as having certain taboos which are universal because they are specifically named in Scripture, Christianity as a universal religion also has certain positive signs by which all men will recognize Christians. Some of these are the fruit of the Spirit: love, joy, peace, patience, kindness, goodness, faithfulness, gentleness, and self-control (Gal. 5:22).

Paul sets another universal example: "Let us therefore, as many as are perfect, have this attitude; and if in anything you have a different attitude, God will reveal that also to you; however, let us keep living by that same standard to which we have attained" (Phil. 3:15-16), as well as:

> Rejoice in the Lord always; again I will say, rejoice! Let your forebearing spirit be known to all men. The Lord is near. Be anxious for nothing, but in everything by prayer and supplication with thanksgiving let your requests be made known to God. And the peace of God, which surpasses all comprehension, shall guard your hearts and your minds in Christ Jesus.
>
> Finally, brethren, whatever is true, whatever is honorable, whatever is right, whatever is pure, whatever is lovely, whatever is of good repute, if there is any excellence and if anything worthy of praise, let your mind dwell on these things. The things you have learned and received and heard and seen in me, practice these things; and the God of peace shall be with you (Phil. 4:4-9).

Above the human culture is a divine pattern which the spirit of redeemed man is to reflect in whatever context he finds himself. Yet the human culture cannot be ignored; it must be faced.

In an unpublished report, Dr. G. W. Peters refers to a conference of missionaries and national pastors who met in Hyderabad, India, to discuss the issue of establishing norms that should guide believers in the adoption of customs that are permissible in the Christian church. Their conclusions present a good pattern for guiding present thinking.

A. Those customs which are essential to the followers of Jesus Christ and for the edification of the Church, such as monogamy, must be adopted.

B. Those customs which are unchristian must be given up. Idol worship, placation of evil spirits, caste, the color-bar, child-marriage, and the degradation of widows, are a few examples.

C. Those customs which are socially expedient should be adopted, even though they be sanctioned by religious beliefs that are unchristian, for such beliefs can be purged. For example, frequent bathing should be continued.

D. Those customs which are socially destructive should be abolished or altered. These include all that put life, health, or happiness in jeopardy.

E. Those customs which are neither unchristian nor socially destructive, may be adopted or reject as desired. Examples are vegetarianism, modes of worship and ritual, postures in prayer and styles of dress.

F. Those customs which are not essential to Christianity nor socially destructive, but which tend to restrict the expansion of the gospel or limit the Christian fellowship, should be abolished. Indianized forms of worship of a Hindu style would give offence to Moslem converts and vice versa.[1]

One final important point should be considered. In the transposition of the message, how much may the form of the

---

1. G. W. Peters, "The Relationship of Christianity to Non-Christian Cultures," Unpublished class notes, Dallas Theological Seminary, 1976.

message be altered in order to convey the content of the message? Some are strongly propounding a dynamic equivalent in order to effectively transmit the message. With all respect to and appreciation for the purpose that is proposed, it would seem that the dangers inherent in such a position are more than may have been recognized. The purpose of communication is to transmit the truth, not to convey an idea. In the transmission of the truth when Scripture speaks of the offering of a sacrifice as in the Old Testament, it gives details of the animals that may be chosen. The animals were chosen because they portrayed certain characteristics. They were culturally symbolical because the culture was formed around the animals. Scripture uses those animals with very definite typological significance. To substitute other animals known to a particular culture is to destroy the original significance, typology, and teaching.

Another way is to teach the recipient group the cultural setting of the Scripture along with the truths of the message. Thus rather than try to interpret Scripture, it is far more preferable to translate the truth and teach the signficance of the truth conveyed. For example, instead of trying to change the sacrificial animal from a lamb to a chicken because the recipient group only know chicken sacrifices, it is far more meaningful to translate the truth, and teach the significance of the point under discussion. We are capable of learning the significance of cultural events of Bible times, and are enriched in our own minds and culture by coming to an appreciation of them. Other peoples are just as capable of bridging cultures as we are. After all, Scripture was not given to the people of the U. S. nor of twentieth–century Europe. It was given to a definite people, at a definite period of history, progressively and meaningfully to each. The truth, revealed within the culture of that time, is universal truth and more fully understood as the context is more fully comprehended. To divorce Scripture from its original setting is to do great injustice to Scripture.

The hermeneutical principle of looking at Scripture in its context cannot be broken by trying to translate Scripture into another cultural context. Scripture does not come under the judgment of culture, but culture comes under the judgment of Scripture.

Bibliography

Coleman, Richard J. *Issues of Theological Conflict*. Rev. ed. Grand Rapids: Eerdmans, 1980.

Guthrie, Donald. *New Testament Introduction*. Rev. ed. Downers Grove, IL: Inter-Varsity Press, 1971.

Jansen, John Frederick, *Exercises in Interpreting Scripture*. Philadelphia: Geneva Press, 1968.

Nida, Eugene A. *Message and Mission: The Communication of the Christian Faith*. Pasadena, CA: William Carey Library Publishers, 1975.

Ramm, Bernard. *Protestant Biblical Interpretation*. Grand Rapids: Baker Book House, 1970.

Rice, Edwin Wilbur. *Orientalism in Bible Lands*. Philadelphia: The American Sunday School Union, 1953.

Ryrie, Charles C. *Biblical Theology of the New Testament*. Chicago: Moody Press, 1959.

Schodde, George H. *Outlines in Biblical Hermeneutics*. Columbus, OH: Lutheran Book Concern, 1917.

Wilkinson, John. *Interpretation and Community*. New York: St. Martins, 1963.

3

The Cultural and Spiritual Mandates

The issue of a cultural mandate versus a spiritual mandate is one that lies at the core of many church and mission policy decisions. It is both a theological and practical issue, in which neither the significance nor the complexity can be minimized. Misunderstanding leads to either evasion of the total mandate or overemphasis of ministry in one direction or the other.

Two Mandates Given

Scripture is very precise in its presentation of two mandates to mankind. The first, Genesis 1:26-28; 2:15. The second, Matthew 28:19-20; Mark 16:15; Luke 24:46-48.

The first mandate was given to Adam as the representative, or head of the human race, while still in his unfallen state. The mandate was, "Be fruitful, and multiply, and replenish the earth, and subdue it: and have dominion over the fish of the sea, and over the fowl of the air, and over every living thing that moveth upon the earth." Then, being placed in the garden of Eden, Adam was given the responsibility "to dress it and to keep it" (KJV).

In this demonstration of confidence in man God made man his vice regent to rule over all creation. Adam was to care for the creation of God. Although Adam would benefit from it, he was to do this for the joy and glory of the Lord who would see the work of His creation cared for in a way pleasing to Him. This was the purpose of the mandate given to man. Thus a special partnership was established. Man was to be coworker together with God to care for God's property. That is, God entrusted a stewardship to Adam, for which Adam was mentally and physically competent. God had, by His creative act, made man capable of performing that which He entrusted to him, and then gave him the privilege of overseeing that enterprise.

This mandate is known as the *cultural mandate* because it relates man to his responsibility to God and over God's creation. It makes him controller of his own environment, as well as executor of a stewardship. This relationship, established between God and man, is one of stewardship. It was a binding responsibility established between Adam, the representative head of the human race, and God the Creator.

Peters well expresses the reality of this mandate when he says in *A Biblical Theology of Missions*:

> The . . . mandate was spoken to Adam as representative of the race and involves the whole realm of human culture. . . . It includes the natural and social aspects of man such as habitat, agriculture, industrialization, commerce, politics, social and moral order, academic and scientific advancement, health, education and physical care. . . . Such culture was to benefit man and glorify God. The Bible expresses it in the following terms: to populate, to subjugate, to dominate, to cultivate, and to preserve (Gen. 1:28; 2:15).[1]

As Genesis records, after the creation of man, sin entered and man fell. As God had forewarned, with the disobedience and entrance of sin, man died spiritually. Further, the earth was cursed and thorns sprang up as a sign of the presence of sin. Still, the mandate to "till the earth . . . with the sweat of thy brow" was reiterated. The mandate was not removed nor

1. George W. Peters, *A Biblical Theology of Missions*, (Chicago: Moody Press, 1972), p. 166.

given to another. Man, who had been made in the image of God, was not made subservient to beast. The orderliness of creation changed, and man's task became harder. Man brought unto himself untold difficulty in ruling over a world that was now in turmoil instead of ruling over a world in harmony. He betrayed the confidence placed in him, yet nowhere does Scripture ever say that the cultural mandate was revoked, or that the stewardship was ever removed or entrusted to another. Instead man's heart became desperately wicked, and the fear of man became evident in the total of living creation. The response of the creatures toward man changed, and fear fell upon both man and beast.

Scripture further records that the cultural mandate was repeated to Noah when he left the ark. Genesis 9:1-3 records:

And God blessed Noah and his sons and said to them, "Be fruitful and multiply, and fill the earth. And the fear of you and the terror of you shall be on every beast of the earth and on every bird of the sky; with everything that creeps on the ground, and all the fish of the sea, into your hand they are given. Every moving thing that is alive shall be food for you; I give all to you, as *I gave* the green plant."

With this statement we find the added factor that now fear should reign between man and beast which did not exist in the Garden of Eden.

Hesselgrave in *Communicating Christ Cross-Culturally* calls this the *social mandate*. He says:

Following the Flood, Noah and his family received promises and a *Social Mandate* that was to apply to them and their progeny down through the generations (Gen. 8:21-9:17). The significance of this simple and sublime story in the first chapters of Genesis must be carefully probed but can never be completely fathomed. It forms the basis of a theology of culture that is amplified throughout sacred Scripture.[2]

2. David J. Hesselgrave, *Communicating Christ Cross-Culturally*, (Grand Rapids: Zondervan, 1978), p. 80.

History records one fact—man has been unable to control the environment and world in which he is living. God created man to have dominion over the earth and to subdue it. Man had the opportunity of harnessing all the powers of nature, all the forces of natural resources, and all the combined potential of the animal and plant realms and to use them to his own ends for the accomplishment of God's purpose. However, with the fall man was condemned to attempt the futile task of subjugating a hostile environment. History has been the continuing saga of man's inability to successfully accomplish the task.

The messianic anticipation, given to Israel, recognizes the futility of the accomplishment of the cultural mandate by man. It holds up a messianic expectation in the prophecy of Isaiah 9:6-7:

> For a child will be born to us, a son will be given to us;
> And the government will rest on His shoulders;
> And His name will be called Wonderful Counselor, Mighty God,
> Eternal Father, Prince of Peace.
> There will be no end to the increase of *His* government or of peace,
> On the throne of David and over his kingdom,
> To establish it and to uphold it with justice and righteousness
> From then on and forevermore.
> The zeal of the Lord of hosts will accomplish this.

Also Isaiah 11:6-9 speaks of the messianic fulfillment:

> And the wolf will dwell with the lamb,
> And the leopard will lie down with the kid,
> And the calf and the young lion and the fatling together;
> And a little boy will lead them.
> Also the cow and the bear will graze;
> Their young will lie down together;
> And the lion will eat straw like the ox.
> And the nursing child will play by the hole of the cobra,

And the weaned child will put his hand on the viper's den.
They will not hurt or destroy in all My holy mountain,
For the earth will be full of the knowledge of the Lord
As the waters cover the sea.

The words of Christ Himself concerning the nature of His mission also include the fulfillment of the cultural mandate, which expresses release from the devastating effects of the fall:

"The Spirit of the Lord is upon Me,
Because He anointed Me to preach the gospel to the poor.
He has sent Me to proclaim release to the captives,
And recovery of sight to the blind,
To set free those who are downtrodden,
To proclaim the favorable year of the Lord" (Luke 4:18, 19).

Thus, in the fulfillment of the messianic kingdom, there will be a restoration of the world to the state that it had before the fall. Whereas in the first Adam the primal state was lost, in the second Adam the original state will be restored.

Edersheim in *The Life and Times of Jesus the Messiah* gives a most interesting insight into the fulfillment of the cultural mandate by Christ. He deals with the miracle of Christ, awakened out of His sleep in the aft of a ship, commanding obedience from the wind and the sea. In this he portrays Christ as the One who fulfills the role which God first entrusted to Adam. He, the second Adam, enters into the exercising of the cultural mandate, and demonstrates dominion over all of God's creation.

"Creation" has, indeed, been "made subject to vanity"; but this "evil," which implies not merely decay but rebellion, was directly due to the Fall of man, and will be removed at the final "manifestation of the sons of God." And here St. Paul so far stands on the same grounds as Jewish theology, which also teaches that "although all things were created in their perfectness, yet when the first Adam sinned, they were corrupted." Christ's dominion over the sea was, therefore, only the Second and Unfallen Adam's real dominion over creation, and the pledge of its restoration, and of our dominion in the future.[3]

Meanwhile, however, though incapable of exercising that right as originally intended because of sin, man is still responsible and accountable for his stewardship over his world. That includes the natural environment, political and social environment with all of the recognized ramifications.

We note the Jews were told, "And seek the welfare of the city where I have sent you into exile, and pray to the Lord on its behalf; for in its welfare you will have welfare" (Jer. 29:7).

Mordecai was commended with the words: "For Mordecai the Jew was second *only* to King Ahasuerus and great among the Jews, and in favor with the multitude of his kinsmen, one who sought the good of his people and one who spoke for the welfare of his whole nation" (Esther 10:3).

So it is that the good of man and fulfillment of the cultural mandate are to be desired and sought after, even while awaiting the eschatological fulfillment.

It is to be concluded, then, that there is a stewardship responsibility resting upon man for the world in which he lives. That responsibility was entrusted to man before the fall, was restated after the fall, and is incumbent upon man as man regardless of his spiritual state. The fall has made the task supremely more difficult. Yet God holds man responsible for the cultural mandate given to him. Even fallen man retains the potentiality and responsibility for faithfulness to his wife, for diligence in the training of his children, for skill in the performance of his daily work, and for justice in his dealings with others. He has the capacity for running schools and hospitals, for tilling the ground and causing even unfertile land to produce. He still has the capacity for governing society. Indeed, it is because of this that God has established a pattern for man's living in this world by ordaining governments to accomplish the cultural mandate. Thus Paul urges all men to obey the governors and pay taxes for the purpose of main-

3. Alfred Edersheim, *Life and Times of Jesus the Messiah*, (Grand Rapids: Eerdmans, 1972), pp. 603-604.

taining cultural and social order in Romans 13. They are ordained to God for the purpose of fulfilling the cultural/social mandate.

Yet the fall has brought man so low in sin that he no longer can function with the perfection that the world order demands. Spiritual death and depravity are evident in every aspect of human endeavor, to the disgrace of man and evidence of sin. However, above it all, God's common grace is evident over all men, so that man is restrained from being what he might be as a result of sin, and enabled to achieve some degree of what God wants him to be. Through it all, a messianic expectation is promised.

The second mandate is known as the *spiritual mandate*, because it relates redeemed man to his spiritual responsibility. It is recorded by Matthew, Mark, and Luke as the mandate of the new covenant. The spiritual mandate was given to the eleven disciples, the representative head of the new creation, as the progressive unfolding of a new truth. It is God's plan for the church, purposeful, all-inclusive, and universalistic in nature. It includes all power, all authority, all peoples and nations. Matthew expresses it, "Go therefore and make disciples of all the nations, baptizing them in the name of the Father and the Son and the Holy Spirit, teaching them to observe all that I commanded you; and lo, I am with you always, even to the end of the age" (Matt. 28:19,20).

Mark stated it, "Go into all the world and preach the gospel to all creation" (Mark 16:15).

Luke confirmed it, "Thus it is written, that the Christ should suffer and rise again from the dead the third day; and that repentance for forgiveness of sins should be proclaimed in His name to all the nations, beginning from Jerusalem. You are witnesses of these things" (Luke 24:46-48).

John rehearsed it, ". . . as the Father has sent Me, I also send you" (John 20:21).

In the statement of the Great Commission, as given in the New Testament, no repetition of the cultural mandate is given. The New Testament command is to proclaim in clear terms the new message of the death and resurrection of Christ to all the world. The Old Testament responsibility was man's responsibility, belonging to all men and never revoked. There was no need to repeat it. The spiritual mandate was given only to the redeemed people. Paul was the great champion of the church, living and proclaiming the spiritual mandate.

At the time of the fulfillment of God's purpose in Christ the need for the spiritual mandate became manifest. Christ came into the world for the purpose of reconciling men unto Himself. Having accomplished His work of redemption, Christ then entrusted to His church the ministry of reconciliation (1 Cor. 15:1-4). The church became steward of the new mandate, committed to the apostles as the representatives of the church.

It is clear then that there are two mandates in force. First, the cultural, was entrusted to Adam as representative of the human race. This has never been revoked, and holds man responsible for his vice-regency over all creation. All men are under it. Second, the spiritual mandate was entrusted to the believers, or members of the body of Christ, the church. It was entrusted to the eleven apostles as representative of the new creation, and holds all members of the redeemed body responsible for its fulfillment.

Two Positions Affirmed

Because of confusion of the two mandates, certain tensions have arisen. The missionary, being an individual of one culture and moving into another cultural world, is faced with the tension of the two mandates, and has to struggle to understand his role in face of the commands to be carried out in a context completely foreign to him. To make matters more confusing, many have never faced the issue and analyzed the complexity of the problem before being faced with it in the new context.

To polarize the tension, the positions may be cited as the social emphasis, and the spiritual emphasis.

The social emphasis has been proposed by liberal theologians, with man's need and present state at its center, bringing justice to all men everywhere. It has focused upon man in society, man in culture, and man in relation to man in both individual and national enterprises. The basis of this emphasis is upon an ethic derived from the human worth of man, and the cultural mandate which says, "Subdue the world; have dominion over it." It requires that man as man establish a relationship between men that is just, ethical, loving, kind, and fulfilling. It considers man as a whole being, and attempts to meet his total need. In essence, it is the attempt to bring in the kingdom of God upon this earth now. It is the attempt to bring fulfillment to man and to the cultural mandate.

This social emphasis fails by not dealing adequately with the results of the fall and its effect upon man. It supposes that man is capable of administering the responsibility, failing to recognize that man, as a fallen creature, is sin-controlled and incapable of performing this function. Many strive in the power of sinful flesh to operate in the false hope of attaining human dignity and control. Fallen man has a capacity for unfaithfulness, for irresponsibility, for carelessness and slothfulness, for lying and stealing, for hate and murder. He has the capacity for working injustice with his neighbor and with society. Every culture gives witness to the fallen nature of mankind everywhere; thus every culture comes under the judgment of the Word of God.

A theology that holds to the fatherhood of God and brotherhood of man without adequately dealing with the fallen state of man is committed to the elevation of natural man, and is destined to frustration and failure in reaching its goals. Man cannot perfect human society himself. He needs help from outside himself.

A second contributing factor to the issue is the amillennial theological position which asserts denial of a literal eschatological kingdom as the fulfillment of prophecy. Its position is the assertion of a present kingdom of God here and now, which is the basis of liberation theology. Standing upon the given premise it is quite understandable that there is great motivation to preach and work toward the fulfillment of the prophecies related to the kingdom of God. If the kingdom characteristics as stated by Christ in proclaiming His purpose in coming (as already quoted in Luke 4:18,19) are to be anticipated now, then most certainly it is the function of the church to bring in that kingdom. With reason, the church then struggles to attain such a world peace, racial rest, social justice, and equality. The fight is a legitimate fight, for it is warfare against the enemy of men's souls and total life pattern. This could (and in some cases does) lead Christians to join hands with communism in the attempt to bring about a kingdom utopia. Consequently, we find the theological liberals, the amillennialists, and the promoters of liberation theology on the side of social emphasis.

The spiritual emphasis camp is composed of the theological conservatives, fundamentalists, and the premillennialists. The extreme position held is that the church has received a spiritual mandate. The fulfillment of the kingdom promises is seen in the future eschatological kingdom which Christ Himself will usher in at His return and, therefore, is not incumbent upon the church. Fulfilling the kingdom promises is not man's responsibility, nor is it the church's responsibility. Consequently, the pertinent mandate is the spiritual mandate—the commission to preach and teach so that as many individuals as possible will be won to the Savior.

The origin of this position may be attributed to the Anabaptists, who saw the world as totally evil, and the only function of the church to seek the called–out ones, separating themselves entirely from the world and its encumbrances. The pietistic and puritanical position with its strong legalism contributed to the continuance and pursuit of such a position. In it the world was seen as doomed, and the only alternative was to preach to the individual, so that those individuals who were the elect might be saved out of the wrath to come. The only concern was for the individual spiritual redemption.

Another contributing factor is the interpretation of prophecy. The premillennialist position holds that the world will grow increasingly worse and worse as the day of the Lord draws nearer. It is therefore futile for man to try to change the course of world history which has already been determined. This leads, in the extreme, to fatalism.

Two Resultant Actions

As a result of the conflict, it is inevitable that two courses of action should be followed. In the debate we only speak of the extremes while recognizing that between the two there are many individuals and groups who have tried to seek a balance.

Sociocultural emphasis

One emphasis is the outworking of a sociocultural application that has developed ministries in areas related to human depravity and need. It considers man as living in the image of God, and capable of controlling his world. It has been directed toward what has been termed the *social gospel*, and in the extreme has reduced the gospel to a social message and the church to a social institution. Great amounts of money have been directed into institutional ministries such as schools and hospitals. Men and women have given themselves unselfishly and sacrifically to incarnate Christ in their lives—to go about doing good as Christ did, to heal the sick, to cleanse the leper, to feed the multitudes—considering that even giving a glass of water in Jesus' name was proclaiming His love. It has led to a presence theology where the fulfillment of the declaration, "Ye are the salt of the earth, ye are the light of the world," is the end.

Out of this has grown resultant involvement in political action to try to right all the wrongs of society, to eliminate racism by supporting revolution, and a whole series of related social actions. All of this has come under the name of mission. The mission of the church has been redefined as that influence which will bring about the kingdom of God in this world.

Spiritual emphasis

The emphasis of the other extreme has been to promote the spiritual mandate as the ultimate and only motive worthy of action. Its pattern has produced an evangelism geared toward individual reaching individual in personal salvation, and the formation of local churches composed of the called-out ones.

The result is that missions commit themelves only to the ministry of reconciliation of individuals. In the history of such perspective any work outside of direct evangelism was justified only in its being a door of opportunity or means to the end of evangelism. Medical ministry was conducted as a means of reaching a patient so the gospel message could be given, not administering aid because the individual himself was worthy of the aid. Education was a means of contact so the gospel could be offered, not because man was himself worthy of education. Agriculture was to be taught as a means of contacting people with the gospel, not because man was hungry and the church had an answer to his problem. Nothing was attempted that was not for the purpose of evangelizing the individual. Very little emphasis was placed upon the fulfillment of the cultural mandate.

Whereas this position, the result of an anabaptistic theology, is presented as the extreme, it is used by some as an accusation against puritanical missiology. In reality one would be hard pressed to find a medical doctor, or a teacher, or an agriculturalist today who actually held such an extreme position. The argument is truly leveled against a straw man that is built up in order to blow him down for the purpose of self-protection. On the mission field and among those actively engaged in missions such a position rarely exists.

In view of the conflict and tension produced by the two divergent positions, there has been a call for redefinition of evangelism. Does evangelism demand a holistic definition which includes the fulfillment of the cultural mandate, or is it the redemption of the soul of man alone? Those who are influenced by a context of oppression are demanding a definition that includes liberation and the fulfillment of the cultural mandate as an integral part of evangelism. They hold that man as man is worthy of redemption, and that evangelism is not confined to reaching his soul alone. Those who operate within a free society are reluctant to accept a holistic definition, turning to 2 Cor. 15:1-4 as the total acclamation, which is the creedal definition of evangelism. The conflict will not be settled until the issue of definition is settled. Separation of definition from context is most difficult, because presuppositions form such a vital part of one's thinking.

Possibility of Harmonization

Although we will not resolve the problem here, the student of missions must be aware and appreciative of the complexity of the problem and sensitive to the divergence of positions.

Redefinition of evangelism

One solution proposed calls for redefinition of evangelism. The problem is that such a call comes out of a context that demands a new definition to answer a felt need. It fails to deal adequately with the Scripture. It errs in the same way that the liberal theological position fails to deal adequately with the fall of man and subsequent depravity and inability to serve as vice regent over God's creation.

Matter of reconciliation

The second proposed solution is that the church commit itself totally to the ministry of reconciliation and let the redeemed body then accept its responsibility for society. It proposes that the redeemed can run hospitals and operate schools; that the redeemed can vote in politics and take part in social enterprises, and thus fulfill the cultural mandate. This solution does not provide sufficient teaching and guidance on these matters to prepare the people of God to perform in these functions. It has proven itself to be too simplistic to cope with the task set before it.

Harmonization of mandates

Another solution seems to be a true recognition that both mandates were to be fulfilled by man, while at the same time recognizing the inability of fallen man to extricate himself from his sinful nature and state. The cultural mandate was given to man, and he is held responsible for its fulfillment; the spiritual mandate was given to man, to fulfill all aspects of man's needs.

Dichotomizing between man's spiritual and physical needs fails to fulfill the intent of the spiritual mandate which is to restore man to his position of being in the image of God.

A harmonization will demand that the church recognize that the cultural mandate was given to man, and the church is still part of humanity and under that mandate. Because man is man, he is worthy of all recognition and support to take him out of the state of decay into which he has fallen, but from which he cannot save himself. He is not to be judged as worthy of his suffering because it is the result of the fall and of sin. That is the state of every man. Such judgment only places the judge in a pharisaical position. Rather, an understanding of the grace of God reveals that man, made in the image of God, is worthy of all love and help because Christ died for him, loving him with an everlasting love.

Understanding the cultural mandate and the reality of common grace bestowed upon all men gives reason for such programs as education, medicine, social welfare, and agricultural projects. This helps man to be and to do what he was meant to be and to do. But this is not the end. A harmonization also demands an understanding of the spiritual mandate. It recognizes that no amount of social welfare will of itself bring redemption. It demands a presentation of the gospel message in love, coupled with action, that communicates the infinite and eternal love of God in Christ Jesus.

Finally, we come to the conclusion: God has given two mandates to the world. The one is a general mandate to all men. The other is a specific spiritual mandate to the church. The church, as the minister of reconciliation and composed of redeemed men, has the *dual responsibility* of fulfilling both mandates. It cannot take a singular position. It has a ministry of reconciliation and a stewardship of sociocultural responsibility.

Van Til stated it clearly when he wrote in *The Calvinistic Concept of Culture*:

> The author is greatly concerned about the alarming resurgence even in Reformed circles today of pietistic withdrawal from

the world and the Anabaptistic denial of the Christian's cultural calling. Granted that the missionary mandate of the church, given in the great commission, ought to be its main concern, how does the believer show himself to be a recruit of Jesus Christ in his daily vocation? Does the twentieth-century disciple have a right to discard the cultural mandate, twice given to the human race by Jehovah himself? Are we justified in turning the world and culture over to the enemies of God? . . . Should not the duty of man become his joy? Is not his task to be undertaken as a privilege? Does not love fulfil the law and thus set man free to enjoy the liberty of the sons of God?[4]

The fact is that the Christian's concern should be to bring culture under the rule of Christ through the power and teaching of the Word of God. Thus the Great Commission itself states: "Go therefore and make disciples of all the nations . . . teaching them to observe all that I commanded you" (Matt. 28:19,20). Is the cultural mandate not part of the "all things?" By this the soul will be redeemed and culture sanctified. The results of spiritual redemption will influence cultural and social aspects of life. The results of the gospel will touch every phase of man's life and being. That is as it should be.

Bibliography

Bavinck, J. H. *An Introduction to the Science of Missions*. Grand Rapids: Baker Book House, 1977.

Edersheim, Alfred. *The Life and Times of Jesus the Messiah*. 2 vol. Grand Rapids: Eerdmans, 1972.

Hesselgrave, David J. *Communicating Christ Cross-Culturally*. Grand Rapids: Zondervan, 1978.

Peters, George W. *A Biblical Theology of Missions*. Chicago: Moody Press, 1972.

Van Til, Henry R. *The Calvinistic Concept of Culture*. Grand Rapids: Baker Book House, 1959.

4. Henry R. Van Til, *The Calvinistic Concept of Culture*, (Grand Rapids: Baker Book House, 1959), p. 22.

4

The Church in
Its Nature and Function

In God's program we are struck by the repetition of a simple pattern by which God has chosen to communicate to mankind. Repeatedly God chose one particular instrument through whom He would reveal universal truth.

In the beginning God communicated to the father of mankind, Adam. Then Noah was God's instrument; Abram and Moses followed, then the nation Israel. In all of God's dealings we have seen His universal care, concern, and provision revealed through His particular chosen means.

Now God has chosen a new instrument, the church, through which He will carry His message of redemption to all the nations. In Christ came the culmination, when salvation was offered to all. As the sin offering He was lifted up on behalf of all. Christ was the One unique sacrifice that takes away the sin of the world (John 1:29). After the death of Christ and His resurrection, God turned to the new body, the church, as His divinely chosen instrument to be His witness and messenger in and to all the world. The church was a body with a new nature, distinct from any previous body that had existed before. It had a new function, distinct from any function performed previously.

That new body is explained by the use of new figures to portray it.

1. The church as the body with Christ as the Head (1 Cor. 12; Rom. 12:3-8; Eph. 4:7-16; Col. 1:18, 24).

53

2. The church as the bride of Christ (Eph. 5:23-32; 2 Cor. 11:2; Rev. 19:7-9; 21:2, 9).
3. The church as the building of living stones with Christ as the Foundation and Cornerstone (Eph. 2:19-22; 1 Peter 2:4-7).
4. The church as the kingdom of priests with Christ as the great High Priest (1 Peter 2:5-9; Heb. 5:1-10).
5. The church as the flock with Christ as the Shepherd (John 10: 1-30; Acts 20:28).
6. The church as the branches with Christ as the true Vine (John 15).
7. The church as the new creation of which Christ is the head as Adam was head of the first creation (1 Cor. 15:45-47; Eph. 4:21-24; Col. 3:9, 10).

These figures portray a reality that is universally understood. God was in Christ establishing a new entity by which His witness to all the world would be carried out. Christ Himself pronounced the truth, ". . . I will build My church; and the gates of Hades shall not overpower it" (Matt. 16:18).

Scripture shows how from the day of Pentecost, just fifty days after the death of Christ, the church was born. It was a new body, designed by God for a distinct purpose, just as Abram, while not yet a Jew, was chosen by God and set apart to be the father of a new nation. God called Abram and made a covenant with him, saying "And I will make you a great nation, and I will bless you, and make your name great; And so you shall be a blessing" (Gen. 12:2). The apostles were told, "And behold, I am sending forth the promise of My Father upon you; but you are to stay in the city until you are clothed with power from on high" (Luke 24:49).

The new body, the church, was a new entity with a divine purpose for which it needed divine enablement. It was in body, a human organ which of itself could do nothing. It was in material, human. But Christ, while of human flesh, being empowered by the divine nature, could do all things whatever the Father willed. So the new body of Christ, made up of human building stones, indwelt by the Holy Spirit, could do all that the Father willed. The church became the living organism through which God would work out His purpose in this age.

It is not our purpose to present a full treatise on the church. That is the labor of many capable expositors and has been amply done. Our purpose alone is to present certain inherent characteristics about the church that must be universally understood if the church is to fulfill her role in the world. Understanding the church in her nature and function will help the missionary understand both her supracultural nature and her cultural role as she is planted in all the world.

Our first question has to do with the nature of the church. What is the church? From a study of the usage of the term *ekklesia* we find that it refers to a body of called–out people. However, with the calling out is also the intent of calling together as the calling of a congregation around some gathering point. The term is thus used to refer to those who are called out of the world by being called together around Christ. The force is more in the center of attraction toward the One to whom they are called than it is in reference to the state left behind.

The calling is a calling of men. It is seen in the response of men who believe God and turn from their old way and belief to follow a new belief and new Lord.

There are two aspects of this new relationship. First is the relationship to Christ that makes all believers part of the church universal, in which all of Christ's followers are members. Second is the relationship between believers that unites them in a local assembly as a manifestation of the universal body. Thus a local church is a local congregation or assembly of men and women who are united to Christ by virtue of their faith in Him, and indwelt by the Holy Spirit through whom the new birth is given.

Scripture presents certain ideal characteristics by which the church is known. They are, by nature, characteristics of the church universal and are the ideal to which every local assembly subscribes. They were the characteristics of the early church as presented in the Book of Acts.

1. Made up of genuine believers, who were indwelt by the Holy Spirit (Acts 2:41, 47; 5:11-14).
2. Observed the ordinances of baptism and the Lord's Supper (Acts 2:41, 42, 46).
3. Acted together as a corporate body (Acts 2:42-47; 4:32).
4. Followed the apostle's teaching (Acts 2:42).
5. Met regularly for prayer and fellowship (Acts 2:42, 46).
6. Cared for the practical needs of its members (Acts 2:44, 45; 4:32).
7. Disciplined its erring members (Acts 5:1-11).
8. Exhibited a corporate, holy, separated, loving, and united lifestyle to the world (Acts 2:42-47; 4:32-35; 5:11-13).
9. Witnessed to the community (Acts 3:11-26; 4:4, 8-31; 6:8-7:60).

In these characteristics the nature of the church became evident. It was a local body, made up of believers who had determined to follow Christ. They all with one mind held worship, prayer, the ordinances, and fellowship as essential. They all sought to follow the instruction of the apostles, believing them to have been ordained of God to deliver the truth of God to them. They endeavored to keep unity of mind, unity of lifestyle, and unity of compassion as their life pattern. They all were intent in living so that their life witness was united with their word witness to reach others for the Lord.

The nature of the church then may be presented in one figure, recognizing it to be an organism, made up of living components, in one united body. See Figure 5.

The center of the organism is Christ, with the Holy Spirit and the Word become alive. Three aspects of the church are provided for its own nurture and growth. These are assimilated through the Holy Spirit's teaching and interpreting the Word, as the body of believers gather for worship, instruction, and fellowship. As the body is nurtured and grows in strength and understanding, it enters into the fulfillment of its purpose in the world: that it may proclaim the truth, demonstrated by life witness—the power of the message, and, through loving service, carry the compassion of Christ to a lost world.

Figure 5
The Nature of the Church

The Church

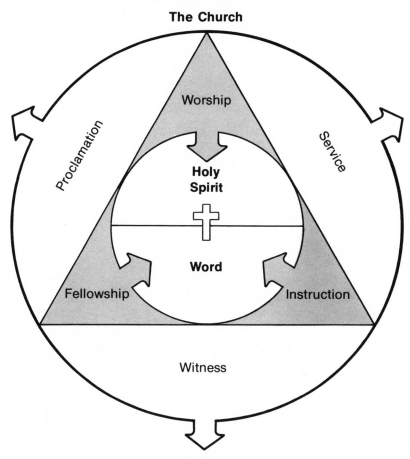

By nature the church is a witnessing body; empowered to witness by the Holy Spirit; alert to witness by its very nature; and able to witness because of its own spiritual life.

These same characteristics may be presented as two sides of a balance (Figure 6), in which true balance is attained in the ideal local assembly.

The one side is given for the nurture and development of the body itself, in order that it might be all that God intends it to be as a witnessing body in the world. The other is the

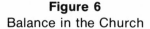

Figure 6
Balance in the Church

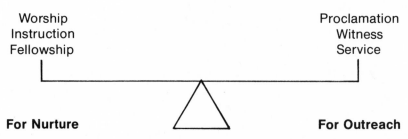

Worship   Proclamation
Instruction   Witness
Fellowship   Service

For Nurture   **For Outreach**

outreach, depending on the nurture for its strength and stability.

In contemplating the nature of the church, Lindsell has well stated:

> Instead of being anthropocentric in nature the Church is theocentric in nature. It is a divinely created and God-willed organization or organism. Immediately we distinguish between the visible and the invisible Church. The invisible Church comprises all believers everywhere without reference to sect or other differences. In it are those who have been redeemed by Jesus Christ. This group of people collectively is called the bride of Christ. It is spoken of as His body. It is called His Church. The visible Church or Churches are the concrete embodiment of the divine institution. . . .
>
> A Church . . . is a communion and fellowship of people who are united in a common faith, having common worship, and a common love. This common worship, and common love revolves around the Head of the Church which is Jesus Christ. The people who comprise the Church are bound together because of the work of Christ and remain together because of loyalty and love to Him. And the church is governed and operated and controlled by the Holy Spirit of God. The people making up this fellowship are called in the New Testament "saints" and "priests" and "sons of God."[1]

1. Harold Lindsell, *An Evangelical Theology of Missions*, (Grand Rapids: Zondervan, 1970), pp. 115-116.

It is out of its very nature that the purpose of the church is seen. Rather than being an organism for its own edification alone, the very nature of the body itself is that it might thus perform the work of the ministry for which it was created. It is the instrument of God in the world on behalf of the world. It is a body of priests set apart to stand before God on behalf of the world, and before the world on behalf of God (1 Peter 2:9).

Bavinck has well expressed it:

> Scripture is quite plain that it is the church, the body of Christ, which forms the organ through which and in which the glorified Christ will reveal his great work of salvation to the world.[2]

Chafer has stated the purpose in these terms:

> Ephesians 2:7, . . . asserts that the major divine purpose is that in the ages to come God may make a full manifestation of the riches of His grace by means of the salvation which He now accomplishes in all who believe.[3]

In nature then we discover that the church is a universal body, made up of all believers the world over, filled with the Holy Spirit, members of the body of Christ, under His headship and rule, and is a living organism.

In form the invisible, universal organism has become visible in the local assemblies of believers who gather together to worship, to fellowship, to learn, and to reach out to the lost humanity with the compassion of Christ, proclaiming the gospel as the good news to man and demonstrating by life witness the reality of salvation in Christ.

George W. Peters, in an unpublished manuscript, has well stated the constitution of the church, as it is seen in its ideal, local manifestation.

2. J. H. Bavinck, *An Introduction to the Science of Missions*, (Grand Rapids: Baker Book House, 1977), p. 59.
3. Lewis Sperry Chafer, *Systematic Theology*, Vol. 4, (Grand Rapids: Zondervan, 1947), p. 45.

The church ideal is constituted out of people:

1. Who by faith have entered a life relationship with Christ. They are believers in Christ;
2. Who have been called out of this world, separated from the world and are God's peculiar possession;
3. Who have been regenerated by the gracious operation of the Holy Spirit. They are born again people, new creations of God;
4. Who have been united by baptism by the Holy Spirit into a living organism with life relations one to another and to Christ who is the Head of the body;
5. Who have been constituted into a brotherhood with family relationships which supersede race, color, language, nationality, denominationalism or any other human barriers or divisions. They are members of the same household of God, children of the same Father, brethren in Christ;
6. Who have been made God's peculiar people to serve God's purposes in this day and age-world evangelism, mutual edification, restraining evil in the world and glorifying God the Father and His Son Jesus Christ. They are the light of the world, the salt of the earth.
7. Who have a unique hope for the ages to come. They are the Bride of Christ who is to occupy a place of uniqueness at His side.[4]

In function the universal church can only be seen in its local demonstration. It is recognized by its adherents, whose lifestyle and proclamation make it a known entity in a given community. The local church is in essence the extension of Christ Himself, reaching out to men everywhere. Christ expressed this purpose when He said, ". . . as the Father hath sent Me, I also send you" (John 20:21). The church became the agent of Christ to fulfill His purpose in the world. Why had

4. George W. Peters, "The Scriptural Definition of the Nature of the Church," nd. pp 5-6.

Christ come? "To seek and to save that which was lost" (Luke 19:10). Why is the church sent into the world? For the same purpose for which Christ came!

Donald G. Miller in *The Nature and Mission of the Church* has well stated:

> Mission is not a special function of a part of the church. It is the whole church in action. It is the body of Christ expressing Christ's concern for the whole world . . . mission is the function for which the church exists.[5]

Franklin M. Segler in *A Theology of Church and Ministry* has expressed it:

> The church was created for the purpose of ministering. Its existence is the shared life of its Lord; its purpose is the shared ministry of its Lord. Although the church cannot rightly be considered an extension of the incarnation, it nevertheless manifests the continuing spirit and purpose of Christ through its life ministry. The ministry of Jesus is the norm for the church's ministry.[6]

Paul expressed it very clearly when he wrote:

> Therefore knowing the fear of the Lord, we persuade men. . . . For the love of Christ controls us. . . . and gave us the ministry of reconciliation . . . and, He has committed to us the word of reconciliation (2 Cor. 5:11-19).

All of the above, considering the nature and function of the church, has been stated in absolute terms in a completely acultural manner. That which Scripture asserts is in terms of absolutes, not subject to cultural norms. It is above and beyond culture, meant for every culture. What God is, He is by His very nature. He is not controlled by, nor subject to, culture.

5. Donald G. Miller, *The Nature and Mission of the Church*, (Richmond, VA: John Knox Press, 1957), p. 69.
6. Franklin M. Segler, *A Theology of Church and Ministry*, (Nashville: Broadman Press, 1960), p. 23.

Likewise, the church universal is, by its very nature, beyond culture. What it is, it is.

In equal manner, the church in its function is an organism designed to perform according to its intent and purpose in harmony and in accord with its nature. In function, therefore, the church is again above culture, and functions according to its inherent purpose, not being dictated by the culture in which it finds itself locally.

However, when we come to the form of any given local body we find it is always incarnate in human flesh living in a cultural environment. Therefore, the church local takes on a cultural expression, just as Christ in the flesh took on a cultural way of life living in Palestine in a given period of world history. This form adjustment must be considered as complimentary to the nature and function.

In dealing with function we must recognize that no body functions in a vacuum. The church is no exception. Though it is spiritual and mystical in its universal essence, that does not change its being a very real body in a very real world. By nature the church is God's agent for the world, and thus very much in this world (John 17:13-18).

As an entity in the world the church is very much a cultural part of the world. The church is not to be controlled by the culture, but to be adaptable to the culture, even as Christ was adaptable to the culture. Christ lived in a specific society and adapted Himself to the pattern of that society, yet without sin. Both literally and figuratively Christ clothed Himself with the cultural clothing. In the same way the church clothes itself with man's cultural clothing. In Asia the believers wear Asian dress. In the West the believers wear western dress. Now the eastern dress and the western dress serve the same essential function. Both are for protection of the body against the prevailing elements, whether heat or cold, wet or dry. Both are likewise for the adornment of the body. But the garments are different.

Is it not to be expected then that the church will take on different clothing according to its environment, and take on different forms of expression in worship, and different forms in its pattern of instruction, and different expression in its fellowship? Further, is it not likely that the form of local church government may also vary according to the patterns of government of a given society?

More of this will be considered in a subsequent chapter, "The Book of the Acts, Principles or Patterns?"

Bibliography

Bavinck, J. H. *An Introduction to the Science of Missions*. Grand Rapids: Baker Book House, 1977.

Chafer, Lewis Sperry. *Systematic Theology*. vol 4. Grand Rapids: Zondervan, 1947.

Costas, Orlando E. *The Church and Its Mission: A Shattering Critique from the Third World*. Wheaton, IL: Tyndale House, 1975.

Getz, Gene A. *The Measure of a Church*. Ventura, CA: Regal Books, 1975.

_____*Sharpening the Focus of the Church*. Chicago: Moody Press, 1976.

Hanson, James H. *What Is the Church? Its Nature and Function*. Minneapolis: Augsburg Publishing, 1961.

Hay, Alexander Rattray. *The New Testament Order for Church and Missionary*. Temperley, Argentina: New Testament Missionary Union, 1947.

Lindsell, Harold. *An Evangelical Theology of Missions*. Grand Rapids: Zondervan, 1970.

McCall, Duke K. *What Is the Church? A Symposium of Baptist Thought*. Nashville: Broadman Press, 1958.

Miller, Donald G. *The Nature and Mission of the Church*. Richmond, VA: John Knox Press, 1957.

Radmacher, Earl Dwight. *What the Church Is All About*. Original title, *The Nature of the Church*. Chicago: Moody Press, 1972.

Scott, Ernest F. *The Nature of the Early Church*. New York: Charles Scribner's Sons, 1941.

Segler, Franklin M. *A Theology of Church and Ministry*. Nashville: Broadman Press, 1960.

Shelley, Bruce L. *The Church: God's People*. Wheaton, IL: Victor Books, 1978.

Snyder, Howard A. *The Community of the King*. Downers Grove, IL: Inter-Varsity Press, 1977.

Stedman, Ray C. *Body Life*. Ventura, CA: Regal Books, 1979.

Stibbs, Alan M. *God's Church*. Downers Grove, IL: Inter-Varsity Press, 1959.

Turner, John Clyde. *The New Testament Doctrine of the Church*. Nashville: Broadman Press, 1951.

5

The Book of Acts:
Principles or Patterns?

A very important decision for missions hinges upon one's view of the interpretation of the Book of the Acts. Is the intent of the author to present the history of the church as a pattern of form for all local churches to follow? Or did Luke present the facts of the formation of the church, universal and local, intending to present principles that would be foundational, but allowing diversity in form according to cultural patterns?

If Luke's intent was to present a pattern for all local assemblies to follow regardless of cultural differences, then truly we should have a church that would be recognized quite easily by its visible form worldwide. It would truly be a universal body in the respect that all local congregations would follow the same form as the apostles established and be united in pattern and structure. This would definitely be one step in the fulfillment of our Lord's prayer, "That they may all be one" (John 17:21).

Looking from an idealistic, simple, rational perspective, it is very natural to assume that God might direct His emissaries to establish a pattern that would be a universal pattern for His church. It would present a universal church that could easily be recognized in all the world. It would serve to unite all believers into one recognized body, and solidify that body into corporate witness. The body would recognize its own members, and the world would recognize the church without confusion.

The ultimate of this would be for all believers to meet in homes, sing and speak in Greek, wash one another's feet, all wear the same Roman dress, the women all wear the same head dress, and greet one another with a holy kiss. Certainly if the church universal did these things it would be a recognized body in the world. The followers of Islam have succeeded quite well in establishing and adhering to a recognized form of identification. Certain cults are readily recognized by their dress and behavior. Following a single pattern, all would be able to worship together regardless of country of origin, and travelers would immediately be at home with those who were Christians everywhere.

If the intent of Scripture is to present one single form for the church then the disparity of form within diverse groups that have set up a variety of church polities and church structural forms is not only opposed to Scripture, it is sinful because it is opposed to God's pattern and is causing confusion in the world. If unity of form is God's pattern, then diversity of structure has produced confusion, destroying the testimony. Only a return to true Biblical form within the church would rectify this confusion and bring about the universal witness that the church was intended to bear.

Returning to the question of the authorial intent, if in fact the intent of Luke was to present foundational principles, then one could expect that the form of local assemblies might differ according to cultural differences. The question is, "How much can a local body of believers adjust to the cultural context and still be the church as Christ intended it to be?"

The same question is asked concerning our Lord's ministry here on earth. Did He give us a detailed methodology to follow in an evangelistic pattern, or did He give us principles to follow?

In response to the question, Robert E. Coleman in his book *The Master Plan of Evangelism* has laid out what he calls the *principles* of our Lord. He states:

> [This study] is an effort to see controlling principles governing the movements of the Master in the hope that our own labours

might be conformed to a similar pattern . . . a study in principles underlying His ministry—principles which determined His methods.[1]

From his vantage point he then lays out eight principles that Christ used:

1. Selection   Men were His method.
2. Association   He stayed with them.
3. Consecration   He required obedience.
4. Impartation   He gave Himself away.
5. Demonstration   He showed them how to live.
6. Delegation   He assigned them work.
7. Supervision   He kept check on them.
8. Reproduction   He expected them to reproduce.[2]

Without doubt we are dealing with a hermeneutical question. We do not have a textual problem and there is no question raised concerning the accuracy of Luke's reporting. Further we have the Epistles of Paul that follow, confirm, and expand the report of Luke in doctrinal teaching.

There is no question concerning the report that Paul confirmed elders in Ephesus. The real question arises over the application of such procedure for all churches in every culture. Elders were known in Ephesus apart from the church. Elders were known in the Jewish synagogue. The question then is asked, "Were elders confirmed in Ephesus as initiating a universal church practice, or was it a form that fit a particular culture, permitting that some other form might serve the same function in a different culture and be equally valid for the church in that culture?" Is the point that *elders* were appointed, or that *leaders* were appointed who happened to be called *elders* in the Ephesian culture?

Certain assumptions are basic to our consideration. First, as described in an earlier chapter, this discussion assumes that

1. Robert E. Coleman, *The Master Plan of Evangelism*, (Old Tappan, NJ: Fleming H. Revell, 1978), pp. 12-13.
2. Ibid., p. 7.

the nature and function of the church are not under question. It has already been stated that the nature and function of the church are established by Scripture, are absolute, supracultural, and outside of our present consideration. Second, it is accepted that the purpose of the study is to determine the author's intent, so that whatever that intent may be it may be followed in practice. Third, discovering that intent will give the missionary direction concerning the form of a local assembly he may establish, and govern the structure and pattern of that body. Fourth, it is recognized that in any case there are limitations on what may be acceptable because all cultures are human and therefore permeated by sin, and all come under the judgment of Scripture so that all forms and practices must be scripturally examined and no sinful practice would be permissible.

A very pertinent hermeneutical question relates to scriptural and apostolic authority. Some have proposed that due to scriptural authority which is binding upon believers today, such authority is binding not only in the area of doctrine but also in practice. Adding the factor that the apostles were specially chosen and instructed of the Lord, their practice becomes both idealistic and normative for the church and believers today. Therefore the pattern initiated by Paul and the apostles was of special significance in giving a binding pattern for the church.

Also to be considered is the factor that being the initiators of a new body which was clearly initiated by the Holy Spirit through His chosen instruments it is only reasonable to expect that the Holy Spirit would introduce a form that would be universally acceptable, and in following that pattern a universal body would be brought into being easily capable of cross-cultural understanding.

There is strong testimony in favor of this application considering the instruction of Paul given to Timothy (1 Tim. 3) and to Titus (Titus 1) which would bear out the intent of appointing *elders* or *bishops*, and to be normative in every culture.

Alexander Rattray Hay of the New Testament Missionary

Union has essentially espoused this position in his study, *The New Testament Order for Church and Missionary*. He states in his preface:

> The only authoritative and complete text-book on church order and missionary procedure is God's Word. . . . Many of God's servants throughout the world are seeking to discover this way [the New Testament way]. There is, indeed, a wide-spread work of the Holy Spirit leading back to the divinely revealed order.[3]

Later in dealing with the church as revealed in the Epistle to the Ephesians, Hay says:

> This spiritual structure, of which Christ is the chief corner-stone, is "built upon the foundation of the Apostles and Prophets." The Apostles laid the foundation—both structural and doctrinal (cf. Acts 2:42)—as it had been revealed to them by the Lord and the Spirit. Peter, in such passages as his sermon on the day of Pentecost and 1 Peter 2:4-9, shows that the foundation is based upon the revelation given to the Prophets. Paul traces it further back still, to God's purpose formed "before the foundation of the world."
>
> The foundation laid by the Apostles was perfect and complete. It was upon that foundation that Paul built. . . . For the practice of New Testament methods and principles of church-planting, it is, of course essential that we return to the true Apostolic foundation.[4]

Reasoning from the apostolic authority some come to the conclusion that when Christ revealed His truth to His apostles and led them by His Spirit He did so in order to establish patterns for His work. Today we accept the statement: "God's work done in God's way will receive God's blessing." If then a missionary wants to see God's blessing on his ministry he will do it in God's way. They say that is the way in which

3. Alexander Rattray Hay, *The New Testament Order for Church and Missionary*, (Temperley, Argentina: New Testament Missionary Union, 1947), p. 9.
4. Ibid., pp. 151-152.

Paul as the first church planter was led, who gave us a pattern to follow.

The well-known champion of the indigenous church philosophy, Roland Allen, says, ". . . people have adopted fragments of St. Paul's method and have tried to incorporate them into alien systems, and the failure which resulted has been used as an argument against the Apostle's method."[5]

Such a position is used to show that Paul's method was with divine direction and that method is to be repeated in all circumstances and countries worldwide.

Just as easily, however, the cultural interpretation would fit. Paul appointed *leaders* in the church, and instructed Timothy and Titus concerning the qualifications of those who were to be *spiritual leaders* of the congregation. Elders were appointed in Ephesus because they were recognized within the social pattern, but those who would correspond in the leadership role and function in another society might perform the function equally well within that society. In such an interpretation the focus is not on *elders* but rather on the qualifications of those who were to be chosen as the recognized *leaders*.

Thus it might be argued that *what* Paul did is basic, or principle. *How* he went about it in detail, and in individual application, may vary, and is related to practice. This would be equal to the conclusion of Coleman concerning Christ's methodology in "principle."

If such be the case, Luke's intent is seen to be twofold. First, Luke as a historian recorded faithfully under the inspiration of the Holy Spirit that which he gathered as historical fact. Second, he presents both basic principle and local application. He demonstrates that the church is to be an orderly, organized body under spiritual leadership, demonstrating and recognized by certain spiritual characteristics. Thus principle and practice are merged in his writing. In no sense does this interpretation violate scriptural intent or teaching.

But what difference does it make to a missionary? It makes

5. Roland Allen, *Missionary Methods: St. Paul's or Ours?* (Grand Rapids: Eerdmans, 1962), p. 5.

a marked difference. In the first case, if the missionary understands the principles laid out in Acts to be a governing pattern, then he will seek to establish a church according to what he perceives the New Testament pattern to be. He will not be looking for patterns which have functional significance within the society or culture in which he is working. He will be looking for strict scriptural patterns to direct the assembly. He will look for *elders* and appoint *elders*, seeking to adhere to the nomenclature, and structure the church according to his perceived pattern. To do so may be to establish a pattern foreign to the culture in which the church is planted. It may soon become a figure of western intrusion within the society, because the image is foreign to the society.

In the second case, if the missionary understands the principle to be the governing factor, and the pattern the cultural adaptation of the principle, then he will seek to determine the basic principle taught in Scripture concerning the fundamental function to be performed, and seek to discover the cultural parallel to adapt the form.

Perhaps an exercise will help demonstrate the magnitude of the problem. In each of the statements in Figure 7 mark whether the intent of the author is for practice for all time in a literal way, or whether there is a basic teaching establishing principle that may be fulfilled in another pattern. After looking at some examples in Acts, it would be well to look at other examples in other writings.

After marking an "X" in the chosen column, try to determine the basic standard by which you made your selection. However, remember that your basic guide for making the choice must fit all examples. Try to state that principle which you used. This is your hermeneutic.

Perhaps one solution may be to consider the questions *What* and *How*? Try the above references by asking "What did Paul or the apostles or new believers do?" Then ask the question "How did they do it?" For example:

Question 1. What did the apostles do?—They elected one to take the place of Judas. That was unrelated to culture. How did they do it?—By casting lots. That was related to culture.

Figure 7
A Hermeneutical Exercise

	Practice to be repeated	Principle to be applied
1. They drew lots (to elect an apostle) (Acts 1:26).	_____	_____
2. Repent, and be baptized (Acts 2:38).	_____	_____
3. Peter and John were going up to the temple at the time of prayer—at three in the afternoon (Acts 3:1).	_____	_____
4. Have seven deacons in the church (Acts 6:3).	_____	_____
5. From time to time those who owned lands or houses sold them, brought the money from the sales and put it at the apostles' feet... (Acts 4:32-35).	_____	_____
6. Prayer and fasting with ordination (Acts 13:1-3).	_____	_____
7. Conduct "laying on of hands" with ordination (Acts 13:1-3).	_____	_____
8. Go first to the synagogues to preach the message (Acts 14:1).	_____	_____
9. Expect miracles and wonders accompanying the preaching (Acts 14:3).	_____	_____
10. Practice circumcision (Acts 15:5).	_____	_____
11. Abstain from eating blood (Acts 15:29).	_____	_____
12. Abstain from fornication (Acts 15:29).	_____	_____
13. Take a vow to cut off the hair (Acts 18:18).	_____	_____
14. "Greet one another with a holy kiss" (Rom. 16:16).	_____	_____
15. A woman ought to have a veil on her head (1 Cor. 11:10).	_____	_____
16. Wash one another's feet (John 13:14).	_____	_____
17. Observe the Lord's Supper (1 Cor. 11:24).	_____	_____

	Practice to be repeated	Principle to be applied
18. Go out to preach two by two (Mark 6:7).	_____	_____
19. "Eat anything that is set before you, without asking questions" (1 Cor. 10:27).	_____	_____
20. Meet in homes for worship (Col. 4:15).	_____	_____
21. Lift your hands when praying (1 Tim. 2:8).	_____	_____

Can you state the principle that guided your decision?

Question 2. What did Peter do?—He preached repentance and baptism. That was unrelated to culture. How were they to do it?—The Jewish culture indicated. It was a known procedure.

Question 3. What did Peter and John do?—They went (up to the temple) to pray. When did they do it?—At the customary (cultural) time. Where did they do it?—At the temple (cultural).

Question 4. What did the church do?—Selected deacons. How many?—As many as were needed to serve the congregation.

Question 5. What did the believers do?—They cared for the needy. How did they do it?—By sharing their possessions.

By asking and answering such searching questions it seems that a pattern emerges. The basic instruction concerning what was done seems to establish a principle that is well taken as a guideline for the church today. It establishes order, purpose, and function. These are all carried out in the function of worship, instruction, and fellowship that form the functional part of the church. Just as clearly emerges the pattern that the how, when, and where were culturally oriented and demonstrate the adaptability of the church to function within any cultural context. These aspects cover such aspects as how the selection of an apostle took place, what was the hour for prayer, how the believers greeted one another, where the believers met, as well as what language the people spoke.

Perhaps the hermeneutical principle to be derived then could be stated as follows: *The authorial intent was to faithfully record the historical account so that the principle of what the apostles did in establishing the church could be readily understood and repeated, while allowing the form of the individual local congregation liberty to conduct the church order in a pattern that would produce the same confirmed function.*

If this is the intent of Luke then we perceive that we have a body of truth, applicable universally in principle, establishing a functioning body that fulfills the nature and purpose of the church within the culture and context where it is planted. Likewise, if this is the intent, then there is no foreignness or strangeness to any true local assembly. It has become the body of Christ within the culture where it resides.

If such does in truth take place, will the church be recognized? Of course it will. It will be recognized by its very nature, and it will be recognized by its fruit. The nature does not change. The function does not change. The fruit it produces does not change. It is only the outward form that changes, germinating in the soil in which it resides.

Now we turn to some of the practices seen in the Acts to examine their relationship to underlying principles.

   I. Acts 1:8
      A. The proclamation
          "But you shall receive power when the Holy Spirit has come upon you; and you shall be My witnesses both in Jerusalem, and in all Judea and Samaria, and even to the remotest part of the earth."
         1. The coming of the Holy Spirit
         2. The disciples becoming witnesses
            a. In Jerusalem
            b. In all Judea and Samaria
            c. To the ends of the earth

B. The environment
    1. Political conformity
    2. Cultural uniformity
    3. Linguistic diversity/Greek superiority
    4. Religious domination
       a. Judaism predominant
       b. Greek philosophy and gods
       c. Roman cults
C. The fulfillment
    1. The Holy Spirit came (Acts 2:1-2)
    2. The disciples became witnesses (2:3-12)
    3. Peter preached (2:14-36; 38-40)
    4. The people responded (2:37, 41)
    5. The church was initiated with 3,000 believers (2:41)
    6. Teaching, fellowship, prayer, worship, and sharing followed (2:42-47)
    7. Miracles followed (3:1-10)
    8. Peter preached (3:11-4:3)
    9. The church was increased; 5,000 added (4:4)
    10. Persecution increased (4:5-20)
    11. The number of disciples increased (6:1)
    12. Local church overseers chosen (6:1-6)
    13. The church persecuted (6:8-15)
    14. The church scattered (8:1-ff.)

We need not further outline the book, the words of Christ were fulfilled as recorded in the book: Jerusalem, Judea, Samaria, uttermost parts.

II. The principle of Acts 1:8
    A. The Holy Spirit is operative
    B. The message is proclaimed
    C. The church is established
    D. The believers are gathered
    E. The witness is expanded
    F. More believers are added

How do these entities operate? Within a given religio-cultural context that dictates the details of the record. Luke has recorded how the details worked out, while at the same time showing the movement of history pointing out what transpired.

The message that is the underlying principle for church expansion today is the message that the Holy Spirit is paramount. The message is to be proclaimed, believers are to join in fellowship, worship, and instruction, and the church is to expand. The socio-religio-cultural context influences the details of the movement.

Patterns of the apostolic church (Acts 2:1-52)

  I. Spiritual patterns
    A. It was a church that knew the presence and power of the Holy Spirit.
    B. It was a church of believers.
    C. It was a church that ordered itself around a God-ordained leadership.
    D. It was a church that proclaimed a clearly defined and relevant message of divine revelation rooted in a historical person, facts, and events.
    E. It was a church of living witnesses.
  II. Cultural relationship
    A. It was a church that permitted itself to be molded into a dynamic functioning community.
    B. It was a church that permitted itself to be constituted into a school of discipleship training.
    C. It was a church that lived in the realm of reality experiences.
    D. It was a church that stood amidst suffering and persecution.

What is the principle then that is established? The principle is that the underlying function is the truth that is intended to be conveyed. The practice, as carried out, is faithfully recorded and demonstrates that the principle was applicable to the culture. In fact, the practice was so aligned with the principle that we have a problem in separating the two.

Naturally this leads to the conclusion that, if the practice of the early church is an acceptable practice within the culture of the recipient group, the practice could be followed without change. The only case, then, where difference would be desirable is in cases where practice would be misunderstood or in conflict with some cultural understanding of the recipient group.

We do not now choose leaders by casting lots. In our culture casting dice is equated with gambling, so we have opted to permit a change of practice so as not to offend. We follow the function and adopt another form of practice. Very few are offended by such an adaptation. Many more would be offended by the reverse order.

Our guiding principle should be formulated by strict adherence to the Biblical principle related to function, committed to execute that which Scripture teaches, allowing liberty in the form that is followed.

Bibliography

Allen, Roland. *Missionary Methods: St. Paul's or Ours?* Grand Rapids: Eerdmans, 1962.

————*The Spontaneous Expansion of the Church.* Grand Rapids: Eerdmans, 1962.

Coleman, Robert E. *The Master Plan of Evangelism.* Old Tappan, NJ: Fleming H. Revell, 1978.

Hay, Alexander Rattray. *The New Testament Order for Church and Missionary.* Temperley, Argentina: New Testament Missionary Union, 1947.

6

Man and His Culture

To understand man is to understand his culture—his language, his logic, his mentality, his expressions, his manner of life, his environment, and his world view—for all of these entities influence man and his makeup. It is through culture that concepts are perceived, and in culture that religion in particular is practiced.

Culture is that reference point which gives direction to life. If those reference points are destroyed man is left to drift on a sea of insecurity. To destroy culture is to destroy a way of life or design of living. To divest man of his culture without offering a functional substitute is to place man into a vacuum where he finds only frustration. Cultural interrelationships are vital to man.

Photographically represented, cultural entities may appear as separate factors (Figure 8).

Functionally all aspects of culture are interrelated (Figure 9).

In that interrelationship we discover that cultural elements divide themselves in three distinct levels: (1) material culture, (2) social culture, and (3) philosophical culture. The material culture involves man and his physical surroundings; social culture involves interpersonal relationships; philosophical culture deals with mental, emotional, and spiritual aspects, which are usually derived from interpersonal relationships and influences. Thus they may be depicted as forming three levels of culture (Figure 10).

Material culture deals with food and sustenance, housing

Figure 8
Segments of Culture

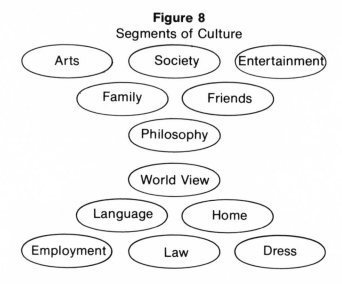

and shelter, tools and handicrafts, clothing, entertainment and economics. Social culture includes family and friendships, interaction in employment and people relationships, and societal placement. Social culture dictates man's place and role, and governs his pattern of life from birth to death. It is social

Figure 9
Interrelationships of Culture

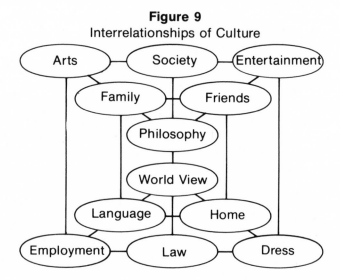

Figure 10
Levels of Culture

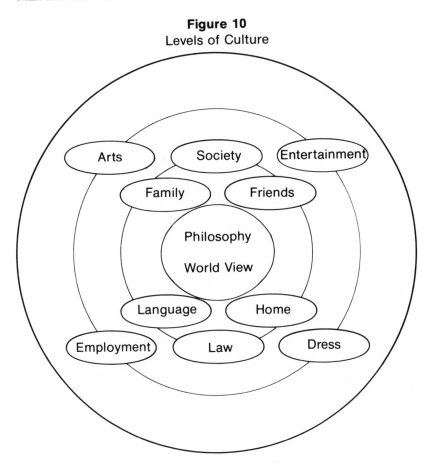

culture that determines the role and placement of the individual in society, and largely dictates status position and symbol.

All cultures maintain family relationships which are the building blocks of society. Interactions within family structure and interactions between family units form an important part of social culture. Privileges, rights, duties, and responsibilities within the social culture all combine to dictate status and role. By understanding these entities related to an individual, one can comprehend the status and role of that individual. One can also determine his own state or standing in relationship to that society. May the missionary beware who does not understand his role and limitations within a given social culture.

Social reference points are age, sex, family relationships, profession, or employment. These factors dictate the social group into which one is relegated. In each culture these same factors hold meaningful significance. By ascribing the role to the individual as the result of applying these references points, his participation in the life and activities of the society is determined. His influence upon society and his ability to be an innovator is also perceived.

In the realm of the philosophical/spiritual it is largely social culture that ascribes a position of leadership role to those who are mental and spiritual leaders, though within each society there are recognized charismatic leadership characteristics. Also, each individual within the group is endowed with mental and spiritual aptitudes. Though these aptitudes may be molded by social dictates, especially formed within the home at an early age, each individual does have his own mental/spiritual capacity which forms part of the individual character. It is the combination of the social culture and the mental/spiritual culture that combine to form the religious entity within culture and within the individual in his culture.

In the sense that religion is used to mean the philosophical, supernatural, and belief systems of people, religion is a universal aspect of behavior. Religion cannot be separated from material or social culture since they all are interrelated and dependent upon each other. The three factors forming culture may be conceived as three cojoining entities (Figure 11).

Within the material there are those aspects which stand almost unrelated to the social, and spiritual/religious. These are the areas in which the missionary is least concerned, because they may be considered to be unrelated to moral behavior. In this category are found such aspects of life as the style of home one lives in, the employment he pursues, and the material possessions he may have acquired. Within the social areas are those aspects of life that deal with interpersonal relationships—his friends, his social status, and his social norms. The law under which one lives is included in this area

Figure 11
Culture Interrelationship

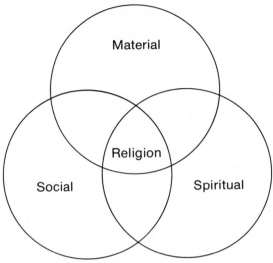

of life, governing much of his behavior patterns. Again much of this is unrelated to moral behavior, though in many aspects it touches both the material aspects of life and the spiritual behavior patterns. Likewise the emotional/philosophical aspects of life have their limits and functions, and there are emotional and philosophical aspects of life which have little to do with the moral/religious aspects. But where the material, social, and spiritual converge to form the world view of the individual is where we find the belief center of the individual, the heart of his moral responsibility. This is where the message of God's Word penetrates into the life of the individual. It unavoidably touches the center of his living and culture.

The point where the three cultural areas converge is that point of greatest strength for the culture itself, and here the individual finds his greatest stability. Material areas may change without seriously affecting the people within the culture, until the change is seen to be affecting the point where the social and spiritual areas are also affected. Then there is resistance to the intrusion. Next, certain social changes may be tolerated, until the encroachment is seen to be influencing the spiritual stability. But Christianity enters to penetrate into the heart of the material, social, and mental/spiritual areas. It penetrates into the heart of that which makes man what he is. Thus the reality of conflict between cultural stability and Christian penetration is unavoidable.

As long as the three factors, material, social, and spiritual, are kept in balance, man's pattern of life remains stable. But when there is movement of one, each of the others is altered to some degree. This pattern of change is universal. There is no society that is not in process of change. The only question is concerning how severely and how rapidly change is taking place.

Of course every missionary is an agent of change, promoting imbalance in equilibrium, and thus promoting change in individual and social life patterns. When the change produced is within tolerable limits the recipients usually have no cause for alarm. They perceive the presence of the individual to be no particular threat. But when the presence of the individual is seen to be upsetting a stable life pattern, then the fear of threat is aroused, and the natural response of protectivism becomes manifest. When concern is aroused then the response becomes energetic, and opposition to the individual becomes apparent.

Within all cultures the "world view" or "religion" of the group is that central element that unites the group. It is the cement that holds the group together. Basically the world view of religion divides itself into four concepts: 1) belief in impersonal power; 2) belief in spiritual beings; 3) belief in many gods; 4) belief in one God, or monotheism.

Belief in impersonal power

Belief in impersonal power is the belief in a magical or essence power which is neither good nor bad in itself, and to which may be attributed any number of characteristics. Such a perception disallows any personality or dwelling, and allows residence in any material object and the causation of any phenomena.

Belief in spiritual beings

Belief in spiritual beings is the belief in souls which are nonmaterial, but real entities, with continued existence. Usually there are degrees of importance, role, and power attributed to each, and fear is also demonstrated according to the power attributed. A natural result of such a belief is the active worship of the spirits or deities by those who hold the belief.

Frequently the souls of the departed are believed to form part of the supernatural realm of spiritual beings, and offerings are made to appease or comfort such ones. At times the concept may be expressed that the spirit of the departed remains with the family, and thus participates in continued life with the living.

Belief in many gods

Where there is belief in many gods, a pantheon of gods is perceived, usually with certain powers attributed to each, and arranged in hierarchical order. Less fear and more worship is usually the pattern among those having a pantheon of gods, with joyful celebrations accompanying the worship of certain favorite deities.

Belief in one God, or monotheism

To those who believe in one God, the personality of God becomes quite definable, as do His attributes and His personal relationship to the world and all that is in it.

The function of religion is to explain the nature of man and the nature of the world in which man finds himself. It serves to give meaning to life and a direction to follow. When a given religion no longer serves its function, a new system is sought which will give stability to man by providing a fixed value system and determinative direction for life.

Value systems form an important part of every culture. Values are ideas, concepts, and practices to which strong sentiments are attached by the members of the society. Values are important in a positive way, and taboos are important in a negative way. People are favorable to strong values, and opposed to negative elements.

American values lie largely in the areas of ambition, industriousness, progress, thrift, and success. We value laborsaving devices, speed and shortcuts, owning our home, being independent. The Hopi Indians value cooperation, not competition. Many nomadic peoples value large herds which are a prestige factor. Among them, programs to prevent overgrazing are totally rejected, because they cut against the very highest value—having large herds. The larger the herd the greater the wealth and prestige. Among some people, large families are greatly valued, and family-planning programs are totally abhorrent because they cut to the heart of the value system.

Values guide the patterns of behavior of any society. Sanctions and rewards are used to encourage the members of the society to follow the accepted patterns of behavior.

In retrospect we discover that any missionary, entering into a culture, is faced with the tension of destroying the equilibrium, and thus is viewed with great caution and suspicion. If he flagrantly moves against either religious system or value system—the very areas of his concern—he is in danger of arousing opposition from the start. Understanding this phenomenon is vital for his own interests and for the message he expounds.

One vital factor to be considered is the area of cultural absolutes and cultural relatives. Cultural absolutes are those aspects of culture which are considered unchangeable. The cultural relatives are flexible. Usually religion is at the heart of the cultural absolutes. Relatives are those areas most influenced by near neighbors that are progressively infiltrating. Likewise there are many aspects of culture that are amoral and of little concern to the missionary. They are those areas of material culture that are farthest removed from the religious: housing, clothing, employment, food and eating habits. They have little to do with moral aspects or with religious practices. In most of these one may quite freely enter, and by this begin to move into acceptance by adapting to the people.

One must not think that adaptation at the material level is unimportant. To the contrary, if one does not satisfactorily adjust himself to the culture at the more peripheral level, how will he win his right to be heard at the next level?

For this perspective, as presented earlier, it is profitable to view the three levels of culture as being concentric (Figure 12).

The missionary desires to reach the religious, which will influence the social and material from the inside out. But he must not forget that his entrance must be through the material and social in order to reach the heart. He must first live among the people to win the right to be heard if he is going to penetrate into the "inner sanctum" of their life experiences.

One of the dilemmas facing a missionary is the judgment factor. Rationalistic anthropologists have presented the thesis that culture is neutral and that each culture determines its own norms of what is acceptable or right, and unacceptable or wrong. Some Bible scholars on the other hand have propounded the position that all human culture is sinful, being the result of the fall of man and consequence of his fallen nature emanating from the utter sinfulness of man and his

Figure 12
Concentric Levels of Culture

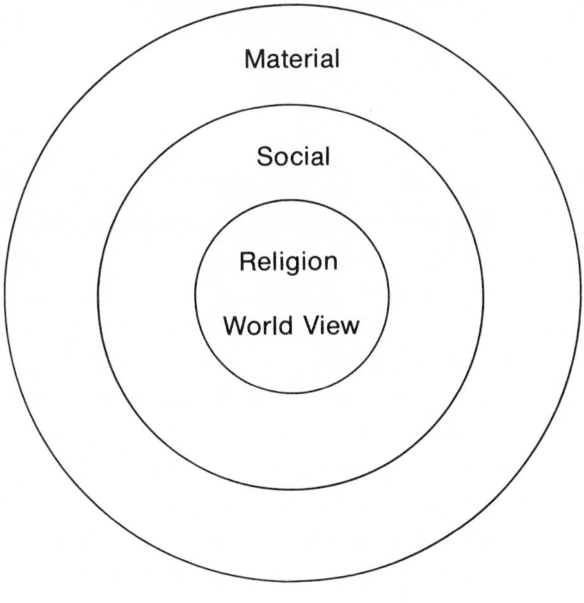

Material

Social

Religion

World View

total depravity. If the first position is accepted then the resulting position must follow that Christianity when presented to any people must adapt itself to the cultural norms of the people. On the other hand, if the total-depravity-of-culture position is taken, then the missionary is bound to denounce all cultural practices as evil and to try to change all cultural patterns. This is what many missionaries have historically tried to do, by transplanting the culture of the missionary as the only acceptable way.

Perhaps a position somewhat between the two extremes is more nearly the Biblical truth. Scripture teaches the depravity of man because of sin, not the depravity of culture. Man has influenced his culture and produced a culture that is contaminated, but not totally sinful in itself. Man may practice evil and defile his environment, within areas where sin and morals affect the surroundings, patterns and lifestyle. But within culture there still remain areas that are not related to sin or morals. Whether a man eats with a knife and fork or with chopsticks is completely unrelated to the sin issue. Whether a man lives in a mud hut with a thatched roof or in a brick home is completely unrelated to the practice of sin. Whether a man is a farmer, or herder of cattle, or employed in a business enterprise is totally unrelated to the problem of sin. Sin may pursue an individual in any of the above, but the employment itself is unrelated to morals or sin. To confuse the issue of the depravity of man by transferring that depravity to culture is to cloud the issue.

Understanding comes when one comprehends the fact that culture is only a way or pattern of life. Man determines his cultural norms. As a fallen creature he adopts patterns that are sinful, destructive, and debasing.

Isaiah clearly portrays the fact in Isaiah 44:14-20. A man plants a tree and it grows. Then he cuts it down. With part of it he bakes his bread and roasts his meat. With part of it he builds a fire and warms himself. With the stock he fashions a god, and falls down and worships it. With the wood there is no evil. With the fire there is no sin. But within the heart of man the evil resides, and the expression comes out in forming an idol from the wood in order to worship it. Sin is in man, not in the wood. But the god made of wood is an abomination.

The answer then becomes clear. God has revealed the nature of man—that is a universal truth. Any object that is an object of worship fashioned by sinful man is an abomination, and cultural acceptance is no excuse. God has pronounced judgment against it (Exod. 20:1).

Scripture, then, has made its pronouncement. All cultures come under the judgment and scrutiny of Scripture. There are practices which are legitimate and in themselves perfectly acceptable. But man, as a sinful creature, has defiled his culture and does not hear or see because his heart is deceived. That is the missionary's concern. The Word of God brings the judgment within the heart of the people.

Early missionaries were offended by the nakedness of so-called primitive peoples, and their first act was to try to change their culture and clothe them before even seeing them come to Christ. Later the pattern changed. Missionaries began to accept people as they were, and ceased trying to change life patterns. They presented Christ and His new hope to the people. When conversions began to take place, then certain cultural patterns, such as putting on clothing, followed. Cultures were seen through new eyes, and the new believers recognized certain practices as evil. Objects of magic and worship were burned or destroyed. Cultures were affected and change entered. The secret was that the light of the gospel began to illuminate men's hearts so they could see the evil and its consequences.

The scriptural response seems to be that the evil is within man. Man has defiled his culture and environment. Much of culture is outside the realm of sin and moral judgment, and is perfectly legitimate to be practiced. Where culture is defiled it is the Scripture that must be judged, not the culture of the message bearer. What Scripture declares to be evil, it does universally. Thus all cultures come equally under the same guiding principles, and common or like practices will emerge within all Christendom. Perhaps these practices will differ in detail and form, but not in function. Thus they will be recognizable universally. For example, dress may differ according to climate and need, but functional covering becomes mutually recognized.

Objects of false worship will be recognized, and the rejection of gods, amulets, and spirit elements will be universal. Where these affect culture, the culture is changed by the innovators of new lifestyles. Thus Christians themselves become the greatest change-agents within a society.

Bibliography

Beaver, Robert Pierce, ed. *The Gospel and Frontier Peoples*. Pasadena, CA: William Carey Library Publishers, 1973.

Belew, M. Wendell. *Missions in the Mosaic*. Atlanta: Southern Baptist Convention, 1974.

Benedict, Ruth. *Patterns of Culture*. Boston: Houghton Mifflin, 1961.

Grunlan, Stephen A., and Mayers, Marvin K. *Cultural Anthropology—A Christian Perspective*. Grand Rapids: Zondervan, 1979.

Hesselgrave, David J. *Communicating Christ Cross-Culturally*. Grand Rapids: Zondervan, 1978.

_____*Planting Churches Cross-Culturally*. Grand Rapids: Baker Book House, 1980.

Kraft, Charles H., and Wisley, Tom N., eds. *Readings in Dynamic Indigeneity*. Pasadena, CA: William Carey Library Publishers, 1979.

Luzbetak, Louis J. *The Church and Cultures: An Applied Anthropology for the Religious Worker*. Pasadena, CA: William Carey Library Publishers, 1976.

Mayers, Marvin K. *Christianity Confronts Culture*. Grand Rapids: Zondervan, 1974.

Nida, Eugene A. *Customs and Cultures: Anthropology for Christian Missions*. 2d.ed. 1954. Reprint. Pasadena, CA: William Carey Library Publishers, 1975.

_____*God's Word in Man's Language*. New York: American Bible Society, 1973.

_____*Message and Mission: The Communication of the Christian Faith*. Pasadena, CA: William Carey Library Publishers, 1975.

Pentecost, Edward C. *Reaching the Unreached*. Pasadena, CA: William Carey Library Publishers, 1974.

Peters, George W. *Saturation Evangelism*. Grand Rapids: Zondervan, 1970.

Verkuyl, Johannes. *Contemporary Missiology*. Translated from Dutch by Dale Cooper. Grand Rapids: Eerdmans, 1978.

7

Man and His Mentality

Every child is born with personal inherent potential, and is individually capacitated and endowed with certain personal characteristics that make him a unique being, different from every other human being. Likewise society and environment begin their molding influence on the individual from the time of birth, making him a part of that society. These influences fall into patterns that affect both the habits and mental processes of the individual. From childhood the babe is taught to do certain things in directed ways, and by that instruction his mind is guided into response attitudes and patterns.

In the West individuality is recognized. School programs are designed for individual learning, and teachers are instructed to encourage the student to advance at his own pace. In the Orient, group learning is much more the pattern. Memorization and repetition are the norm for learning. Children will sit and repeat words, phrases, and arithmetic problems. Thus a group-learning procedure molds the learning process and produces mind sets.

There is no doubt but that mental patterns are learned through the communication process. Society and environment direct the molding procedure. A child of Korean parents must be taught to speak Korean. If he is adopted at birth by Americans and is raised in the U. S. he is totally a U. S. individual with language, learning, and mental activity totally conformed to his social environment. Only his Korean facial characteristics betray him.

We may state that there are physical environmental factors, social environmental factors, and closely related psychological and spiritual factors, that influence an individual's mindset. Thus the physical, or social, psychological, and spiritual environments largely determine the mentality of the individual.

Mentality is not to be confused with intelligence. Intelligence is ability to think and learn. Mentality is a way or manner of thinking and learning. It deals with thought processes, not mental capacity. It determines one's point of view, and his response to given stimuli.

Mentality is closely related to world view. The world view of the nonwestern people with their open, imaginative, and intuitive mentality often baffles and even frustrates the Westerner. The nonwestern world view is often naturalistic in the philosophical sense, distinguishing little between the human and the divine or the material and the immaterial. In this perspective the cosmos is an all-inclusive whole. Because of the tendency towards a participation mentality, fantasy and hallucinations are as real to these people as facts and events are to the Westerner. Dreams and visions are considered just as real as true experience.

The importance of understanding mentality, as it concerns the missionary, is found in its relationship to communication and the communication process. To enter into effective communication one must comprehend, or at least be aware of, different mental processes and perspectives. To communicate the gospel meaningfully, one must recognize that different aspects of an individual are affected. The communication process touches all areas of one's life, and calls for an understanding and response in each area (Figure 13).

The follower of Islam has a problem with the Christian teaching concerning the Trinity and the sonship of Christ. This is a physical problem for him as well as a spiritual or religious one. His mindset is that Allah is One, and he accuses the Christian of having three gods. His concept of sonship cannot be separated from physical intercourse; that is impossible for

Figure 13
Communication Relates to Life

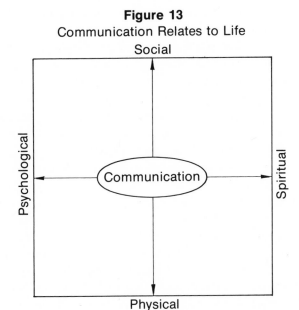

God. Therefore he rejects Christianity at the first level, because it is untenable and impossible for him to conceive.

The Asian operates with a mental perspective of the Yin - Yang concept (Figure 14).

The Oriental perceives of his world as being made up of two forces, ever in balance. While the Westerner perceives of his world as either-or, the Asian perceives equally the both–

Figure 14
Yin-Yang Concept

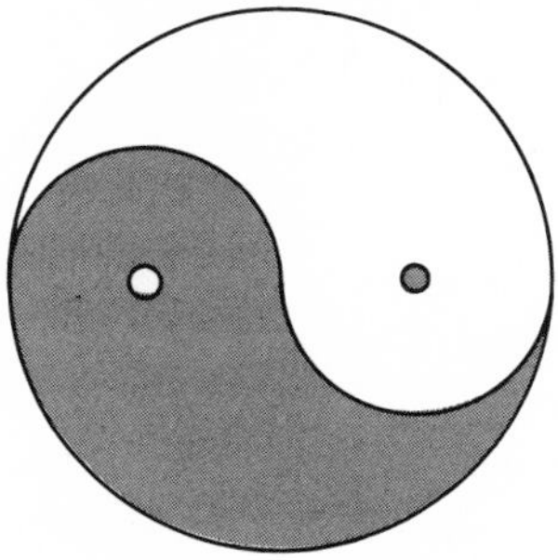

and concept. In the West a thing may be either hot or cold, wet or dry, white or black, right or wrong. In the Asian perspective it may be both hot and cold, wet and dry. These are relative terms. Likewise right and wrong are relative terms. At one time an act may be right, while at another it may be wrong. Within the Yin is always the seed of the Yang, and within the Yang is always the seed of Yin. Thus when Christ is presented, it is very tenable for the Asian to conceive of accepting Christ and holding on to his own religion. Religious pluralism is very convenient and acceptable. One may hold on to both Buddhism and Christianity. Within Buddhism is the seed of Christianity, and within Christianity is the seed of Buddhism. The amalgamation fits a thought pattern without any conflict. Consequently when an Asian is told of the uniqueness of Christ, and that Christ is the only Way, he is offended at the Western mentality reflecting and communicating superiority to the Asian.

Western mentality has been developing a sense of logic for many generations. Logical thinking is dominantly linear in its development. In the West communication patterns follow the logical—linear pattern. An exposition usually begins with a topic statement, followed by logical subdivisions of that topic, each supported by examples and illustrations. The logical subdivisions lead to a conclusion that presents a truth or proves a point.

Thus the Western mentality may be presented as an arrow with important control points on its shaft (Figure 15).

The Mideastern mentality, demonstrated by Old Testament references, frequently operates in parallelisms, often with a positive and a negative. They may be reviewed as follows:

1. Synonymous Parallelism: The balancing of thought between the first and second phrases.

> "I cry aloud with my voice to the LORD;
> I make supplication with my voice to the Lord.
> "I pour out my complaint before Him;
> I declare my trouble before Him" (Ps. 142:1-2).

Figure 15
Western Mentality

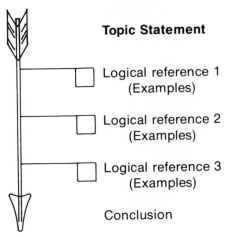

Topic Statement

Logical reference 1
  (Examples)

Logical reference 2
  (Examples)

Logical reference 3
  (Examples)

Conclusion

2. Synthetic Parallelism: The completion of thought in the
                            second phrase.

> "The Lord is my shepherd,
> I shall not want.
> He makes me lie down in green pastures;
> He leads me beside quiet waters" (Ps. 23:1-2).

3. Antithetic Parallelism: Contrast of thought presented
                             in the second phrase.

"The heavens are the heavens of the Lord;
But the earth He has given to the sons of men" (Ps. 115:16).

4. Climactic Parallelism: Suspense until the final phrase
                            completes the thought.

> "How blessed is the man who does not walk in the counsel
>   of the wicked,
> Nor stand in the path of sinners,

Nor sit in the seat of scoffers!
But his delight is in the law of the Lord,
And in His law he meditates day and night" (Ps. 1:1-2).

Asian thought pattern operates more in circular or conical
pattern, as opposed to the linear of the West. A thought is
expressed, and then expanded, then restated, and further
expanded. The thought is repeated each time new factors are
added. This fits with a cyclical world view that allows repetition and expansion, and is congruous with a view of
reincarnation.

Asian mentality may be illustrated as a spiral (Figure 16).

The American Indian pattern of storytelling is very similar
to the Oriental. He will begin telling a story, and make certain
references to his point, then return to his narration repeating
his story with embellishment and more application, until finally
he comes to the point and conclusion. See Figure 17.

Since mentality, culture, and communication are so intimately interrelated, it would seem only reasonable and obvious
that every missionary would study, along with his language
pursuit, the history, geography, society and religion of his
target people. Language itself is significantly more than the
words which are only the vehicle for communicating thought.
Inherent in the words is a wealth of mental perspective that
is vital to accurate understanding. Added to the words is the
nonverbal expression which is often more communicative than
the words themselves.

Through language we transmit awareness, information,
knowledge, understanding, and feeling. Language is the

Figure 16
Asian Mentality

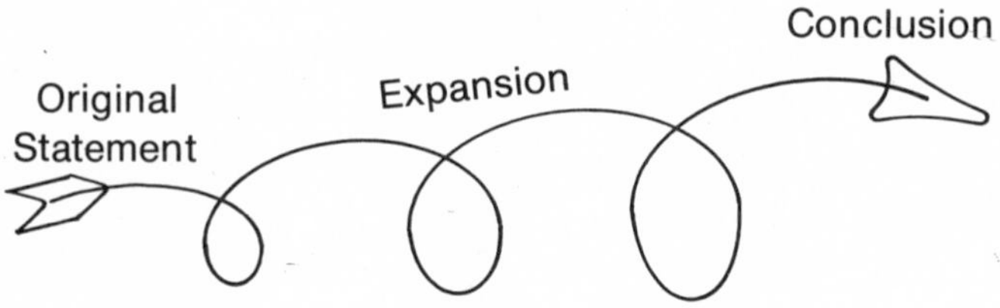

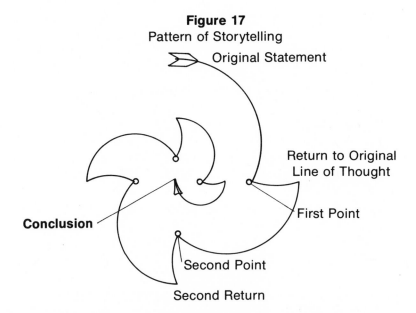

Figure 17
Pattern of Storytelling

expression of the thoughts of the mind and the feelings of the heart. Through it mental perceptions are transmitted. Language patterns that are taught at an early age mold the mind into thinking in these patterns. Then, the language expressions reflect the mindset of the speaker.

For example, when in the U. S. a person waiting on guests at a table accidently spills a cup of coffee, he says, with great embarrassment, "Oh, I am so sorry, please forgive me, I spilled the coffee." This is recognition of guilt and expression of apology. In other places the same occasion elicits the use of the reflexive, which might be translated, "It slipped." Thus the implication is that the individual involved is not to be blamed, because the coffee slipped. In the first instance, blame and responsibility are recognized; in the second, they are transferred.

Since the missionary is vitally concerned about the target individual understanding his message, he must be equally intent upon understanding the mindset of his target group so as to be able to communicate with understanding. Thus the

Figure 18
Comparative Analysis

Western Mentality	Nonwestern Mentality

1. Dynamic
   Always creating.
	1. Conservative
	   Always repeating.

2. Factual
   Preoccupied with detail,
   given to creedalism.
	2. Mystical
	   Fantasy, meditation.

3. Causative
   Always asking "why?"
   Explorative, discovery,
   scientific.
	3. Phenomenal
	   Content with the
	   observable
	   Recognition of natural
	   causes.

4. Creative
   Producing self-suffi-
   ciency, self-reliance, and
   self-determination.
	4. Intuitive and imaginative
	   Producing emotional
	   and mental acceptance
	   and response.

5. Individualistic
   Free enterprise.
	5. Communal
	   Family enterprise, tribal-
	   ism, nationalism.

need to understand the broader concept of language is vital, probing much deeper than pure grammar or words.

Along with language comes the question of mental perception related to concepts. Don Richardson in *Peace Child* related how the Sawi were intrigued with Judas as he related the story of the betrayal of Christ. In their mentality the traitor was the greatest hero, and they were delighted to see how Judas had successfully betrayed Christ. The intended message was lost because of the mindset of the people.

A comparative analysis of different mentalities may be helpful. They serve as stimuli and generalities, but could in no way be applied universally. See Figure 18 as drawn up by Victor Cole, a Nigerian.

Western Mentality	**Nonwestern Mentality**
6. Universalistic Broad world concept.	6. Tribalistic Traditional, confined world concept.
7. Business-oriented Capitalism Time consciousness.	7. People-oriented Socialism Personality consciousness.
8. Dualistic World view: Sacred vs. secular	8. Holistic World view: related to whole of life.
9. Utilitarian The world is an object which man controls.	9. Ontological Man is a small part of the cosmos, subject to its laws.
10. Volitional Man expresses his own will and lives under the control of that will.	10. Emotional Man lives according to his emotions, and gives expression to his feelings.
11. Goal and success oriented.	11. Existence and subsistence oriented.

The initial factor that needs to be recognized is the fact that people are different. Culture, language, geography, history, social customs, social structures, and religion all affect thought patterns. Thought patterns are expressed in linguistic patterns which include both verbal and nonverbal expressions. The expressions must be understood in order to appreciate the communication process, and capture the mentality of the individual.

For the missionary the most important factor is to recognize that there is a close relationship between mentality, which is a learned pattern of thinking, and religion, which is a learned belief and practice. The Hindu and the Buddhist both believe in reincarnation, a very reasonable belief within a meditative mindset that accepts identification with the eternal as most desirable and sought after. Likewise, communal living establishes a pattern for communal decision making rather than individualistic interest. Thus the whole conversion process is related. The imaginative, rather than the logical, may produce more conviction in the heart of the hearer, leading him to action, whereas the logical would leave him unaffected and unresponsive. Our western way is to say salvation does not depend on emotions. We want an individual to understand what he is doing when he accepts Christ. But we fail to understand that the way to understanding for him is through his emotions. He comprehends with his emotions and comes to Christ with heart response, not head response.

Another example of the different mentality is demonstrated in the gift-giving practices. In the West, when one gives a token gift to another he will normally make some comment such as, "Oh, it is nothing, just a little remembrance." He is communicating verbally that he has not sacrificed much for it, and does not wish the recipient to feel indebted by receiving it. On the contrary, when an Asian gives a present he will frequently tell how much he has worked to make or attain the gift. His mind-set is that he wishes the recipient to know how much he appreciates him. To give a gift that cost little would be an insult, implying that the person was not worth much. Therefore it is necessary to convey the value of the gift, to show due appreciation to the one to whom the gift was given.

A second factor to be recognized is that interests vary as mentality varies, and effective communication depends on captivating the interest in order to captivate attention. Minimal communication takes place when interest is not present. Along with the different mentalities and interests goes the relationship of time and place for certain topics of discussion.

In the West many business transactions take place on the golf course. Little of religious conversation takes place with one behind his desk, with a telephone, a calculator, and a dictaphone before him. But that same individual may talk freely at a "breakfast" or at a private home conversation.

As a young missionary in Mexico I thought I could provide a good setting for personal evangelism. I bought two season tickets to the symphony with the intention of inviting a friend to the concert each week. My plan was that after the concert we would stop at a restaurant and have a bite to eat, and the friend would be ready to listen and talk of spiritual things. It did not take long to discover that one did not mention either politics or religion in a public place such as a restaurant. The mentality dictated by social custom drew a barrier to such topics of conversation.

Finally, mentality affects the encoding and decoding processes in communication as well as the time, place, and method of sending and receiving messages. To be able to communicate effectively one must consider the mentality factor of those involved. That is a learned art, but an essential element of effective communication. More of this appears in the chapter "The Communication Process."

Bibliography

Dale, Kenneth. *Circle of Harmony: A Case Study in Popular Japanese Buddhism with Implications for Christian Mission*. Pasadena, CA: William Carey Library Publishers, 1975.

Dayton, Edward R., and Fraser, David A. *Planning Strategies for World Evangelization*. Grand Rapids: Eerdmans, 1980.

Gulick, Sidney Lewis. *The East and the West: A Study of Their Psychic and Cultural Characteristics*. Rutland, VT: Charles E. Tuttle, 1963.

Hesselgrave, David J. *Communicating Christ Cross-Culturally*. Grand Rapids: Zondervan, 1978.

Manikam, Rajah B. *Christianity and the Asian Revolution*. New York: Friendship Press, 1954.

Moore, Charles A., ed. *The Chinese Mind: Essentials of Chinese Philosophy and Culture*. Honolulu: University Press of Hawaii, Eastwest Center Press, 1967.

_____*The Japanese Mind: Essentials of Japanese Philosophy and Culture*. Honolulu: University Press of Hawaii, Eastwest Center Press, 1967.

Nakamura, Hajime. *Ways of Thinking of Eastern Peoples: India—China—Tibet—Japan*. Rev. ed. Philip P. Wiener. Honolulu: University Press of Hawaii, Eastwest Center Press, 1964.

Richardson, Don. *Peace Child*. Ventura, CA: Regal Books, 1974.

Waddy, Charis. *The Muslim Mind*. New York: Longman, 1976.

8

The Communication Process

Effective communication is the art of transmitting a message from one individual to another in such a way that the message is received with a minimum of distortion or dilution. Verbal symbols compose the major portion of the process, but intonation, emphasis, and context all contribute very significantly to the process as well.

In written communication the words become the only channel of conveyance. Therefore, the writer either assumes the reader understands the context, or he has to use words to further explain the context. Otherwise the reader is left to his own resources concerning what the influence of the context might be. In verbal communication, the intonation, voice emphasis, and gestures indicate the context and intent which aid in the interpretation of the message.

Figure 19 depicts a situation in which two individuals, speaking the same language and operating within the same cultural context or field experience, communicate with each other. The communication is clear to the extent that there is mutual understanding of the words used. Where there is lack of understanding of words and expressions, there is lack of communication.

Two medical doctors may converse with each other and maintain a high level of communication. Two engineers in the same field may communicate with a high degree of proficiency. But a doctor and engineer may find that their level of communication is minimal in their respective spheres of

Figure 19
Intracultural Communication

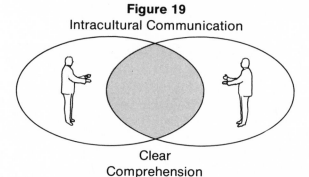

Clear
Comprehension

expertise. The reason is that their context, vocabulary, and understanding of each other's field of reference is so foreign that comprehension is significantly reduced.

Figure 20 depicts the compounding of the problem of accurate communication due to the expanding of the linguistic and cultural differences between two groups or individuals. As seen in the chapters "Man and His Culture" and "Man and His Mentality" language, cultural elements, mental perspectives, and psychological perspectives influence the context and, thus, both the expression and interpretation of language. Cross-lingual and cross-cultural communication face complicating factors which reduce comprehension between two individuals.

The known context of communication is also vital to understanding. When two individuals interact within an area known to both, then communication can be maintained at a very high

Figure 20
Cross-Cultural Communication

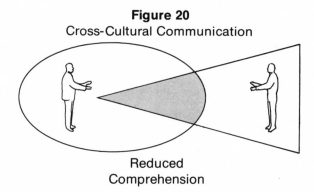

Reduced
Comprehension

degree of precision and exactness. However, when the contextual background or understanding of the two is very diverse then the degree of communication and comprehension is very limited.

Stating the problem in terms of mathematical equation one might say that communication potential is directly proportionate to the degree of similarity in language, culture, mentality, and context. In *Communicating Christ Cross-Culturally* David Hesselgrave provides a diagram of the various dimensions of cross-cultural communication (Figure 21).

Eugene Nida in *Message and Mission* has presented the most simple diagram in which he states that the communication process consists of three essential components (Figure 22).

Figure 21[1]
Dimensions of Cross-Cultural Communication

Culture X	Microculture	Macroculture	Culture Y

World Views—ways of perceiving the world

Cognitive Processes—ways of thinking

Linguistic Forms—ways of expressing ideas

Behavioral Patterns—ways of acting

Social Structures—ways of interacting

Media Influence—ways of channeling the message

Motivational Resources—ways of deciding

Source Encodes Message

Message Decoded by Respondent

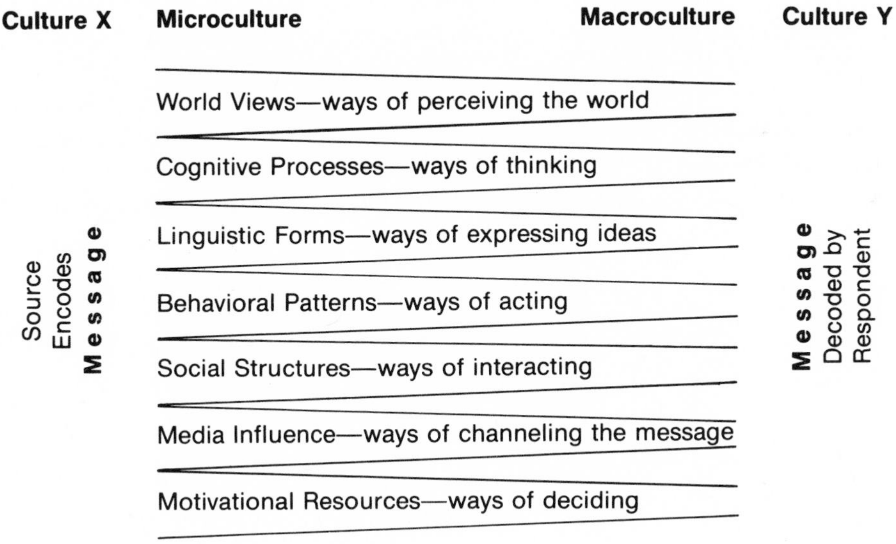

1. David J. Hesselgrave, *Communicating Christ Cross-Culturally*, (Grand Rapids: Zondervan, 1978), p. 97.

Figure 22

S   M   R

The **Source**   The **Message**   The **Receptor**

He sets these three factors within a cultural framework, and makes the S M R congruent with the culture in which they operate. Thus he presents a simplified pattern of communication which is the normal, daily conversational pattern (Figure 23).

However, when a cross-cultural situation occurs then the first problem arises. The cultural context is different, which implies interpretational factors. Also the linguistic differences cause changes. We then have to make a decision. Is the sender to alter his communication pattern, or is the recipient the one to make the adaptation? Where does communication best adapt, and how?

Does one discover a true transmission of the message through a direct transmission process, in which the △S△ △M△ △R△ is exactly the same as in the larger △△ and original context? (See Figure 24.)

Or does one proceed to a complete change of the three elements according to the cultural change (Figure 25)?

Figure 23[2]

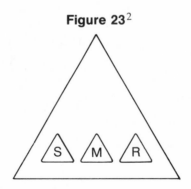

    2. Eugene A. Nida, *Message and Mission: The Communication of the Christian Faith* (Pasadena, CA: William Carey Library Press, 1975), p. 36.

Figure 24

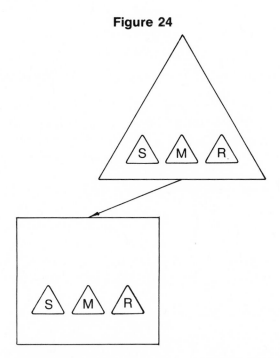

Or does something between the two actually take place, as depicted in Figure 26?

Since the sender is the one who knows best the message he has to communicate, it is his responsibility to do all that is within his power to make the expression as understandable as possible to the recipient so that he may know how to interpret it correctly. The burden for accurate transmission rests upon the sender.

Likewise, when the same message is to be communicated to a third language and context it is the responsibility of the new sender to do all within his power to transmit the message with all clarity possible to the new recipient. Inherent in the process is an unavoidable transmission problem. However, comprehension of the problem can assist in proper care so as to avoid unnecessary confusion.

Nida presents a very simple picture of the ideal (Figure 27). The problem is that /S\ is not │S│ but /S\ in culture │ │,

Figure 25 [3]

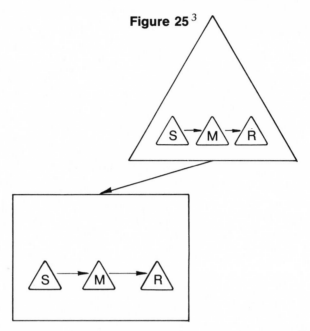

who tries to identify himself with culture ☐ and become ⬠ S , but in reality he becomes △S , a complex of △ and ☐ . To the degree to which △S can void himself of his own culture and adapt himself to the borrowed culture he can become a more effective communicator.

For the individual, then, communication becomes a learned art. Some may have more of a gift for adaptation than others. Some people are naturally better imitators than others. But all can learn, to some degree, the art of adaptation. It is becoming to the transmitter of God's message to be the best adaptor possible.

When God determined to transmit His eternal message to man, He did so in man's language, and within man's culture so that man could understand it. He spoke neither in a heavenly language nor in the language or culture of angels. God transmitted His message in man's language and culture. Every word chosen was the word God wanted, to communicate the

3. Ibid., p. 47. p. 39

Figure 26

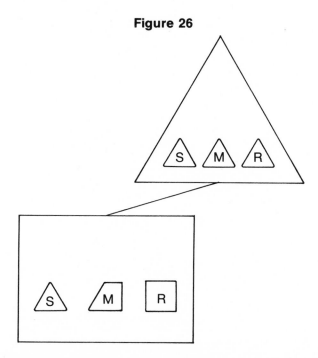

concept He wanted communicated in the context of the human writer. It employed the process of transmitting mental concepts through verbalization of those concepts into intelligible word and phrase symbols so that the concepts could be understood by the recipients in exactly the way they were intended. Thus men who knew not God could understand the message God had enunciated through the human writers in the context of those emissaries.

Effective communication presupposes:

1. That communication is possible
2. That all men do communicate
3. That there is a universal process involved

Effective communication takes place when the message is received by the recipient with a minimal degree of distortion.

One may declare: "The flag is red." The recipient hears and

Figure 27[4]

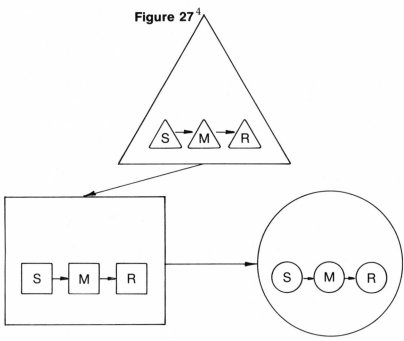

understands: "The flag is red." Effective communication has taken place, though it may not be complete. The degree of redness may not be the same for the sender and the recipient. But the degree of redness or shade of redness is not a part of the declaration, neither stated nor implied. However, if one declares, "The flag is crimson," then there are implications inherent in the word *crimson* and the recipient must know the meaning of the term *crimson* if he is to understand. But, if the sender is the one responsible for effective communication then he must be aware of what crimson means to the recipient or he will send a false message. Effective communication means the transmittal of the message with a minimum of distortion. It is not the emission or proclamation of a message, but the reception that counts.

Elements that influence the reception of a message are:

Language

Idiomatic usage

4. Ibid., p. 47.

Contextual familiarity

World view or field of experience

Psychological frame of reference

Mental attitude

Significance of the message

When an individual wishes to communicate God's message, he must first ask the question, "How well do I understand it?" If he does not understand the message well, he will not be able to transmit it well. Second, he must ask the question, "How well do I understand the recipient?" If he does not understand the recipient's language, idiomatic usage of language, context, world view, psychological frame of reference, and the significance of the message to him, he will send a message but not communicate effectively.

It has been stated that the missionary is not a postman, but an ambassador. He does not deliver a message that is signed and sealed, but rather carries a message that is translated into the language and context of the recipient, in order that the recipient may understand it.

In this form of transmittal the credibility of the communicator is implied. Effective communication does not reside in the message alone. It resides in both the sender as originator and in the credibility of the carrier. Herein lies an important element in the cross-cultural communication of the message. If the originator is not seen as a valid source, then the message will be rejected. Likewise, if the carrier of the message is not credible then the message will also be rejected.

Why did Christ spend his life of thirty-three years on this earth? He lived among men to prove Himself credible before them so men would have the proof they needed, and would receive the message he proclaimed.

This brings us to God's communication to man. God has a supracultural, or rather a supranatural, message to communicate, ⟨M⟩ He put that message into a form adaptable to men's culture △ and through men communicated that mes-

Figure 28

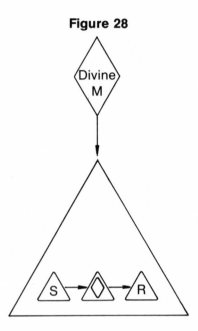

sage to a given culture: Hebrew to the Old Testament people, Graeco-Roman to the New Testament people. Thus we have men, inspired of God, writing exactly what God wanted them to write in terms that could be understood by men within the same culture (Figure 28). The divine message was transmitted to men within man's culture, through chosen men of God. And since effective communication depends on the communicator transmitting his message in terms that are understandable to the recipient, we can have confidence that God communicated exactly what He knew man could understand. The message was still a supranatural message, couched in particular culture symbols. When the communication process then ensues, the communicator must take into consideration the fact that the message is not of human origin, and must recognize that the carrier of that message must be an ambassador who himself is faithful to the message and to the transmittal of the message. In Figure 29 the $\triangle$ R (Receptor) of one culture carries the divine message to a second culture, and tries to interpret that divine message to a recipient of the second culture without distortion of the original message.

Perhaps this seems confusing. If so, think of the recipient of the new message, that is not within his frame of reference or experience, that is not seen as relevant to him, that comes in an unfamiliar language, that often is not carried by a credible agent, and completely opposed to his context and way of life, and you will understand something of the problem of effective communication that faces the missionary. You will understand why the missionary must spend so much time earning the right to be heard, as well as learning not only the grammar of language, but idiom, custom, thought patterns, and studying felt needs of the people.

The divine message can be communicated only in terms understood by the recipient, and this aspect of communication must not be overlooked. Effective communication is not synonymous with proclamation. One may proclaim a message that is completely intelligible to him, but he has not communicated that message effectively until he has transmitted

Figure 29

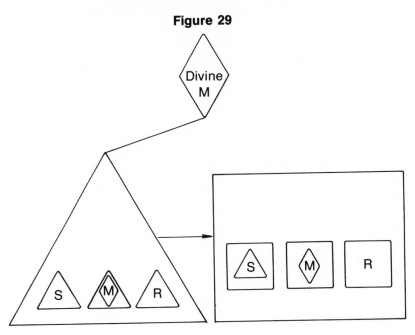

the message in terms the recipient understands—linguistically, culturally, mentally, and spiritually.

Until now we have said nothing of the confusion that enters into the process. In the transmission of a message distortion enters through definition changes, translation difficulties, cultural mores, and mental concepts, to say nothing of the religious practices and concepts. All of these elements pose problems to clear transmission and become barriers to effective communication. These barriers cannot be eliminated. They must be dealt with and overcome. As a construction engineer or architectural designer often tries to make use of a huge boulder that cannot be moved, either as a foundation piece or as an ornamental element in his design; so the cross-cultural communicator tries to take advantage of the cultural elements rather than trying to fight them.

Elements of a culture may be bridges for effective communication rather than barriers. The secret is in learning how to best acknowledge the favorable elements and appropriate them to the best advantage.

Certainly there are elements of every culture that come under the judgment of Scripture. But a premature attack against those elements before credibility is established will only result in a high degree of static that will cause rejection of the messenger before the message is even transmitted.

Understanding the communication process will lead the missionary to study the recipient group, to consider the communication process from that vantage point, and turn his attention to transmitting the divine message in terms that are comprehensible to the group. He will understand that language, culture, context, mentality, and spiritual comprehension all form a part. But he will move with a confidence that communication is possible. All men do communicate, and there is a universal basis through which he can operate.

Bibliography

Dennet, Herbert. *Christian Communications in a Changing World.* London: Victory Press, 1968.

Hall, Edward T. *The Silent Language*. 1973. Reprint. Westport, CT: Greenwood Press, 1964.

Hesselgrave, David J. *Communicating Christ Cross-Culturally*. Grand Rapids: Zondervan, 1978.

Kraft, Charles H. *Christianity in Culture*. Maryknoll, NY: Orbis Books, 1979.

_____and Wisley, Tom N., eds. *Readings in Dynamic Indigeneity*. Pasadena, CA: William Carey Library Publishers, 1979.

Moore, Charles A., ed. *The Chinese Mind: Essentials of Chinese Philosophy and Culture*, Honolulu: University Press of Hawaii, Eastwest Center Press, 1967.

_____*The Japanese Mind: Essentials of Japanese Philosophy and Culture*. Honolulu: University Press of Hawaii, Eastwest Center Press, 1967.

Nakamura, Hajime. *Ways of Thinking of Eastern Peoples: India-China-Tibet-Japan*. Ed. by Philip P. Weiner. Honolulu: University Press of Hawaii, Eastwest Center Press, 1964.

Nida, Eugene A. *Customs and Cultures: Anthropology for Christian Missions*. 2d ed. 1954. Reprint. Pasadena, CA: William Carey Library Publishers, 1975.

_____*God's Word in Man's Language*. New York: American Bible Society, 1973.

_____*Message and Mission: The Communication of the Christian Faith*. Pasadena, CA: William Carey Library Publishers, 1975.

Rogers, Everett M., and Shoemaker, F. Floyd. *Communication of Innovations*. 2d ed. New York: Free Press, 1971.

9

The Conversion Process

By understanding the nature and process of conversion, we can better accomplish the work of evangelization. Confusion concerning the nature of conversion and lack of understanding of the process of conversion contribute much to the discouragement that comes to missionaries in seeing so many of their converts falling away. Erroneously equating a conversion experience with regeneration can lead to misunderstanding, confusion, and frustration.

The Term

The word *conversion* has a broad connotation. Basically it means to turn around; . . . to bring over from one belief, view, or party to another. It always involves a reorientation of the person's values and actions. It begins in the mind and is demonstrated in attitudes and actions. It involves responses and change concerning views and behavior.

Conversion means a change of direction with a total reorientation of outlook and objectives. Perhaps Figure 30 will serve to illustrate the meaning: it is the same individual, but according to his direction his world view is completely changed.

As used in Scripture the primary meaning of conversion is "to turn around." It is the Greek word *epistrophe* used in Matthew 9:22, "But Jesus turning . . . said." It is used in Mark 8:33, "But turning around . . ." and in Luke 1:17, "to turn the

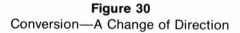

Figure 30
Conversion—A Change of Direction

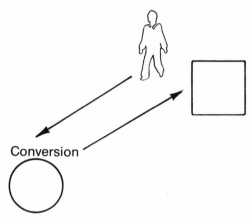

Conversion

hearts of the fathers." Paul uses it in 1 Thessalonians 1:9, "turned to God from idols" and John in Revelation 1:12, "I turned to see the voice that was speaking with me. And having turned I saw . . ."

At times the word appears to be equated with regeneration as in Mark 4:12, "lest . . . they should be converted," (KJV) and John 12:40, "and be converted, and I heal them." However it must be recognized that the concept of turning around fits the context equally well in each of these cases.

Often the word carries the connotation of repentance. The word is used together with repentance in Acts 3:19 where Peter calls the multitude to "repent . . . and return." This conveys the idea of changing one's mind and adopting another view.

Further it is vital to recognize that the conversion process is a psychological process, vital to the makeup of each individual. The experience of conversion is as diversified as individuals, and the relationship to cultural context is as real as the relationship between an individual and his culture.

Finally, conversion to Christ means a change of lords within, following after a new Master, indicating a total change of commitment.

The Perspectives

Focusing on conversion as a process, there are three views which in some aspects overlap and duplicate each other.

The crisis-conversion perspective

The crisis perspective of conversion identifies the exact moment of conversion, equating it with the moment of regeneration. It is viewed as being that moment when an individual knowingly receives Christ and becomes a new creature in Christ Jesus. Paul is the outstanding example of this kind of crisis experience. The Philippian jailor and the Ethiopian eunuch are other examples of the same. In each of these cases the intellect, the emotions, and the will were all involved. There was an intellectual understanding, an emotional response, and a willful act, at a definite point of time.

This kind of response leads some to say, "People are always able to specify a moment when they experienced first forgiveness." This statement equates conversion with forgiveness.

Others place great stress on knowing the moment of conversion in order for the person to have assurance of his salvation. The statement is made, "How can one be sure of his salvation if he does not know the moment of his conversion?" Such a position equates conversion with salvation, a demand which the Scriptures do not require, but which might be simultaneous as the previously mentioned cases prove.

Care must be exercised not to equate words that are not equal, even though the two might occur simultaneously. Nor must certain outstanding examples lead one to conclude that in them we find an unalterable or universal norm or pattern.

The concept of crisis conversion/regeneration might be illustrated as in Figure 31. When the individual is intellectually convinced, he responds emotionally and willfully follows Christ. At the same time, by believing in Christ, he moves into a new relationship with Christ, and is regenerated. His conversion and his regeneration are simultaneous. This for him has been a moment of decision. He will probably long remember the actual moment. Such a perspective views the

Figure 31
Crisis Conversion/Regeneration

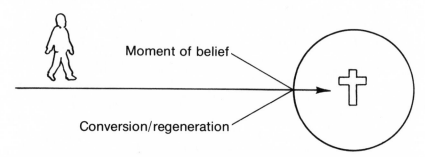

experience as a point in time when the line between belief and unbelief is crossed over. It is truly the moment of forgiveness, and the moment of the new birth.

For many who are in Western Christianized society, the matter of conversion is seen as a point on a continuum. The individual has been born into a professing Christian home or society and all his life he has been moving toward Christ and God. Yet at a moment he becomes aware of his personal need, and publicly announces his personal decision to accept Christ. This act is termed *conversion* in modern usage, though no real act of turning around was evident. It may be stated more accurately that he reached a goal toward which he was heading. In reality, such a pattern fits his psychological mind–set, and his human experience for which he had been conditioned. This does not make his salvation less real, but it does put it within a context for which the individual was psychologically and emotionally as well as culturally prepared, and therefore the exercise of his will was not a difficult decision. In fact, it might have been more difficult for him to act otherwise, because his conditioning and peer support were all focused on such a determined course of action. His direction had been headed that way all the time; he did not pass through a turning around experience, but through an entering in experience.

Of course he did turn around in that he was spiritually headed for condemnation while outside of Christ because of his sin, even though he was within the influence of a Christian home. His turning to Christ resulted in his spiritual rebirth. In this he did experience a true conversion, but the course of his visible life was not altered. It only progressed further in the same direction in which he was headed.

Frequently this process follows a pattern. Preconditioning has taken place rather slowly and constantly. Home life or peer attitudes have provided a constant influence. Then at a given moment the individual is confronted with the decision and he determinedly decides to follow Christ personally. He is truly regenerated and becomes a child of God. His conversion is the result of determined persuasion and action. His conversion and regeneration are simultaneous.

The gradualism conversion process

Although recognizing the reality of the crisis conversion as a viable experience, the gradualism perspective views the process of conversion as a continuum of receptivity to the claims of Christ. Each individual can be categorized by one of the terms in Figure 32.

Figure 32[1]

Gradualism Conversion

+7	Participation	
+6	Identification	
+5	Acceptance	
+4	Association	
+3	Inquiry	
+2	Sympathy	
+1	Interest	
—	**Neutrality**	—
	Suspicion	−1
	Aloofness	−2
	Evasion	−3
	Resentment	−4
	Rejection	−5
	Hostility	−6
	Persecution	−7

1. George W. Peters

In this view conversion is interpreted as the process of moving from the extreme of persecution toward the end of full participation. Thus if a person were completely hostile to Christianity and committed to destroy believers and were to experience a change that would bring him to give up his hostility and at least listen to the claims of Christ he would have turned around in his attitude and moved from the − 7 position to perhaps the − 1 position. He would still be suspicious, but he would have progressed a long way from his previous − 7 persecution attitude. This is the kind of experience many missionaries see occurring in individuals.

It must be carefully noted that an individual who has progressed to the + 1 level on this scale is not yet regenerated. He has not yet accepted Christ or Christianity. Yet, the term *conversion* would apply because he has turned around from his previous antagonistic position and action. This is very easily confused with regeneration by one who sees the change, and wishfully equates the decision with the conversion of Paul. This is conversion in the sense of turning around but it does not yet bring the individual to the position of acceptance of salvation.

In some churches, especially in Latin America, there are groups known as inquirers and sympathizers. These are individuals who are willing to attend services, and willing to learn more of Christ and the gospel, but they are not recognized as church members. They have not given testimony of having accepted Christ personally. Often baptism is that sign by which such an individual is asked or required to give public testimony of his personal faith in Christ. Many of these individuals have moved from the initial − 1 SUSPICION position to the + 3 INQUIRY or + 4 ASSOCIATION position. They would not yet be considered as + 5 ACCEPTANCE or as belonging to the group. In Latin America this is a clear distinctive, recognized by both believers and unbelievers.

John Taylor in *Growth of the Church in Buganda* and Donald McGavran in *Understanding Church Growth* have discussed this view of gradualism conversion. They see five stages in the way unevangelized peoples are converted.

1. *Introduction stage,* in which a missionary wins the right of a hearing. He first must become familiar with the language, culture, and customs in order to become acceptable to the people.
2. *Presentation stage,* in which the missionary begins to present the gospel message. In this period the view of God is elevated and distinguished from the myths of the past. People begin to respond and listen to the proclamation.
3. *Demand stage,* in which the missionary begins to make the demands of the gospel known. This raises a sin consciousness to see their old ways in contrast to God's revealed will.
4. *Answer stage,* in which God's response to man's sin is presented and the group is presented with the person and claims of Christ, and in which each individual is faced with the costly choice. Now the decision is called for.
5. *Instruction stage,* in which those who respond to the claims of Christ are instructed in the meaning of the new life in Christ.[2]

Tippett in *Verdict Theology in Missionary Theory* calls stage four the *verdict.* He sees the need for a clear decision, where ". . . the old things passed away; behold, new things have come" (2 Cor. 5:17).

James Engel has proposed another scale which indicates direction and degree of movement toward Christ and active participation in His body (Figure 33). It too is a continuum.[3]

Such a diagram helps one comprehend the process, and understand how an individual may be categorized at any given stage. Understanding these steps can help a Christian witness know where a person is, and when he has come to the point

2. John V. Taylor, *Growth of the Church in Buganda: An Attempt at Understanding* (1958; reprint ed., Westport, CN: Greenwood Press, 1979) pp. 43-59.
3. C. Peter Wagner and Edward R. Dayton, *Unreached Peoples '79* (Elgin, IL: David C. Cook Publishing 1978).

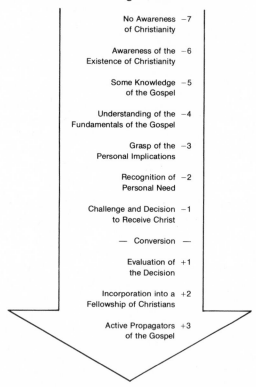

Figure 33
Where Is This People in
Their Movement Toward Christ?
The Engel Scale

of decision. Failure to comprehend the process will lead one to think that a person has decided to accept Christ when in reality he has passed only to another point on the continuum.

How does gradualism work? In many cultures men do not have a concept of personal moral sin because they have no knowledge of the moral nature of God. When this is the case, the missionary must begin with the moral nature of God as revealed in the Old Testament. Once the individual understands the nature and character of God and the sinfulness of mankind, the next step of enlightenment is an awareness of the remedy for sin.

The process proceeds from initial awareness of the gospel to a recognition of personal sin and a decision to act. The person can act favorably or in rejection. The rejection, rather than necessarily being final, can simply be a reverting to a previous point in the continuum to gain more information or perspective. This reverting, in relation to the continuum, should be recognized by missionaries as common and should be welcomed as an opportunity for further clarification.

Believers who have proceeded cautiously and deliberately along the continuum are often those who mature more rapidly because of a sure foundation. At regeneration the process of gradualism shifts from the convicting to the sanctifying ministry of the Holy Spirit.

The psychological conversion perspective

While recognizing the reality and validity of both the crisis conversion and the gradualism conversion processes, one must also contemplate the psychological conversion as a real phenomenon.

The psychological conversion is a very real experience, which involves a true right about-face. It is worthy of recognition. In fact, it is vital that a missionary understand its nature and potential, while also being aware of its danger.

While a psychological conversion may take place, and often does, as a result of a crisis in one's life, it is not necessarily so. There are those who profess spontaneous conversion at the moment of an accident, or sickness, or family trial. There are others who gradually undergo psychological changes and demonstrate a new attitude toward religion, church, believers, and Christ. Such individuals undergo an emotional change that demonstrates a complete turn around. They have experienced a conversion. Attitude and actions may both change radically.

Figure 34 demonstrates such a phenomenon. It illustrates a person who is walking away from Christ and at a given time turns about in his attitude and conduct. It may be that he turns from persecution to a new attitude of tolerance. It may have been brought about through some crisis in his life, but

Figure 34

Conversion Reflected in Changed Attitudes & Actions

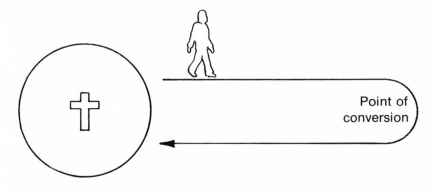

Point of
conversion

whatever the cause may have been, the individual, instead of walking away from Christ and His church, turns around and begins his movement toward the One who has called him. He has not yet arrived at the point of becoming one of Christ's own body, but he has changed his direction, manifest in an attitudinal change.

In reality this moment of change of direction may be called *conversion* because it is a complete turn around and can easily be confused with regeneration. However, it is necessary to recognize that while this may be the moment of regeneration, as in Paul's case, it is not necessarily so. One may change his direction and still be far from salvation. To say that he is born again may be premature, and failure to comprehend this may account for many dropouts. This may be called by some a *false conversion,* and it is in the spiritual sense.

Leininger, in "The Dynamics of Conversion," says of the psychological conversion, "This represents the experience of the person who is transformed in his self-concept and his relationships, who begins to move in a new direction, but has no real concept of a transcendent power in his life."[4]

The experience of psychological conversion is a real expe-

4. C. Earl Leininger, "The Dynamics of Conversion: Toward a Working Model," in *Perspectives in Religious Studies,* Vol. 2, no. 1.

rience. The end may be true conversion when it is brought to culmination, but the experience may lack the dynamic of true regeneration.

The psychological aspects of conversion are very pertinent but too extensive to include in an introduction of the subject. Such a study would cover the how of conversion, the why of conversion, the when of conversion, the where of conversion, and the what of conversion. It would cover the causes and the consequences of conversion. It would include not only conversion to Christianity, but also conversions to other religions. Obviously, this is not the purpose of this study. But it is important that missionaries and students of missions consider the psychological aspects of conversion and be prepared to recognize both their virtues and their dangers.

The Process

At this point a missionary will do well to consider the culture and mental processes of the recipient. Usually Christians in western society place man on a continuum where he proceeds from point 1 to point 5 (Figure 35).

Our culture process carries the individual through a straight-line pattern of reasoning. The mind moves in a rational sequence of events from a starting point to a positive conclusion. Many other cultures, however, carry one through a circle or spiral process. The individual is given a truth, frequently in story or narrative form. Then the story is repeated, and another element introduced. Again it is related with other details. At a point in the process the hearer says, "I see, go on and tell me more." He has progressed to a given position, and responded, but not yet arrived at the point of understanding, or commitment, or acceptance. He is in the process of learning, or turning around, but he may not yet be regenerate.

Figure 35
Linear Pattern of Reasoning

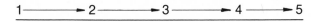

Figure 36
Circular Pattern of Reasoning

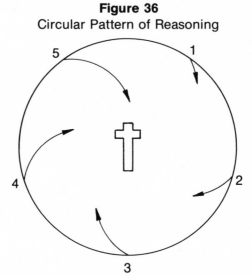

Figure 36 illustrates this pattern. A story is begun and little by little points are added until finally the whole story with its applications is revealed. Not until the whole story unfolds is there total response, though at every point there is response to that point.

In the spiral process, which is similar, the individual is brought through a process of reasoning or learning that depends on his comprehension. It leads the individual from the known to the unknown, including repetition and building. Thus it satisfies the gradual conversion process by leading him ever closer to a decision point. The spiral process is illustrated in Figure 37.

In all of these, the real task of the Christian worker is to determine where in the continuum or circle or spiral the target person fits. He must tailor his ministry to the individual at the individual's point in progress. He must be careful not to extract a premature profession while calling for a verdict. Yet, he must not fail to bring him to the point of decision.

The Elements

The conversion process is not a spiritual matter alone. It is a cultural and psychological process as well. Man is a total

Figure 37
Spiral Pattern of Reasoning

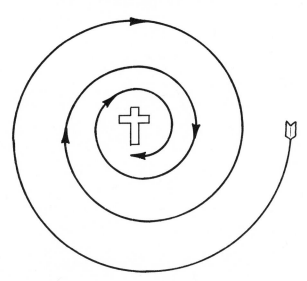

entity living within a context which includes his religious beliefs, his views of the physical world, his social relationships, his psychological framework, and his educational or learning context. The conversion process includes all of these factors as they influence his thinking and acting pattern. (More will be seen in the chapter "Man and His Mentality," but these all influence his conversion process.)

An understanding of the elements of the conversion process must also give due recognition to substitutes for an individual's values. To say, "What will you do with Christ?" may be too simplistic. The individual must be confronted with a whole series of questions, and must know how Christ answers his need in each area of his life.

A human hand may illustrate various aspects of one's total life (Figure 38). He has religious needs, material needs, social needs, psychological needs, and educational needs. To turn to Christ, one looks for answers in each of the areas. A willful decision to follow Christ comes from a satisfactory response to each need.

Another pattern is the wheel (Figure 39), where the indi-

Figure 38
Various Aspects of Man's Life

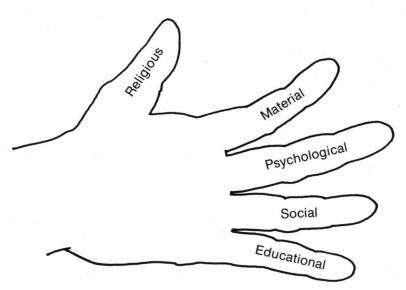

vidual is the hub. He looks from his center on many areas of his life. He contemplates the cost, and has a difficult decision. Understanding the complexity of this decision can give the missionary added patience and sympathy for such an individual.

The Boundaries

In our western perspective we set boundaries on the Christian that are very determinative. We say one is converted when he conforms to certain standards. Those standards seem to be well defined. We feel they are Biblical and we often proof-text our position. We talk about the church as a circle with a well-defined circumference (Figure 40). Those who are within the circle are the redeemed. Those outside the circle are the lost. This approach fits the western culture beautifully and we accept it without challenge.

But we go further. We also recognize that not all within the

Figure 39
Relationship of Man to Various Aspects of His Life

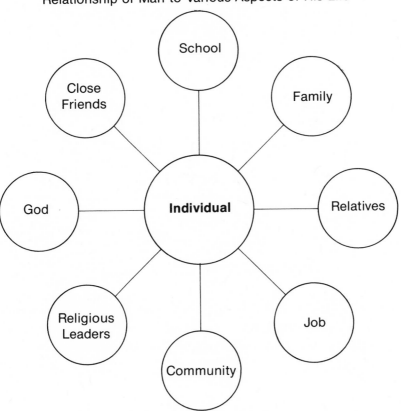

organized church are redeemed. Therefore we put a circle within the circle (Figure 41).

May it not be that Christ's church is not quite so statically defined? May it be that God's grace reaches out more to one who understands less but who has truly turned from his direction of walking away from God to a direction of walking toward God? An example would be the Pharisee who knew much about God but was determined to walk away from His Son in open rejection, as compared with the undeserving sinner who knew little about God but was turned toward Him (Figure 42). The truly converted was the one who in heart and intent set his eyes on the Lord to pursue after Him. Such a

Figure 40
The Redeemed and the Lost

representation of the true body of Christ may be less bound-
ary oriented than our western orientation would cause us to
accept.

Conclusion

We must recognize that regeneration is the end of a process.
Conversion is the act of turning around and may be concurrent
with regeneration, or may be only a change of direction still

Figure 41
The Redeemed and the Lost

Figure 42
The Redeemed and the Lost

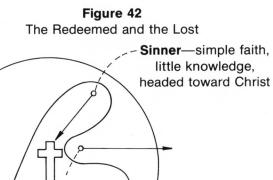

Sinner—simple faith,
little knowledge,
headed toward Christ

Pharisee—much knowledge,
headed away from Christ

far removed from understanding salvation. But regeneration itself takes place at a given moment in time. Conversion may be a process, but regeneration is not.

The process of conversion entails many facets of life and takes place in many different ways in varied individual situations. A missionary's understanding of the process will enable him to cope with the frustrations that otherwise would lead him to total despair. When working cross-culturally the timing for calling for a decision is crucial. There is the tendency to seek a profession before the person is ready. The lack of response or apparent rejection is often treated as final, when in reality the person is still willing to proceed to the next step. His rejection may indicate lack of understanding, or lack of sufficient repetition to meet his decision-making process demands. Or he may be truly converted while still a great way off in his intellectual understanding. The missionary should therefore consider carefully the process and be alert to its demands within the culture and among the people with whom he is working. If he is not sensitive to this he may end up in total frustration and despair.

On the other hand, we must sound a note of warning. By not expecting regeneration to occur simultaneously with conversion the missionary could confuse the new believer. To distrust his salvation when he is genuinely regenerated would be as erroneous as prematurely considering a person to be saved when he in fact was not truly saved. A sensitivity to the work of the Holy Spirit is essential for the minister of the Lord as an agent and instrument used of God.

Bibliography

Kevan, Ernest Frederick. *Going On in the Christian Faith*. Grand Rapids: Baker Book House, 1964.

Leininger, C. Earl. "The Dynamics of Conversion: Toward a Working Model." In *Perspectives in Religious Studies*. Vol. 2, no. 1. Murfreesboro, NC: Chowan College, Fall 1975.

McGavran, Donald A. *Understanding Church Growth*. Rev. ed. Grand Rapids: Eerdmans, 1980.

Stott, John R. W. *Christian Mission in the Modern World*. Downers Grove, IL: Inter–Varsity Press, 1976.

Taylor, John V. *The Growth of the Church in Buganda: An Attempt at Understanding*. 1958. Reprint. Westport, CT: Greenwood Press, 1979.

Tippett, Alan R. *Verdict Theology in Missionary Theory*. Pasadena, CA: William Carey Library Publishers, 1973.

Wagner, C. Peter, and Dayton, Edward R. *Unreached Peoples '79*. Elgin, IL: David C. Cook Publishers, 1978.

10

Change and Accommodation

The only place where people do not change is the place where there are no people. Change is a characteristic of humanity. Individuals change while going through the life cycle. They move from the infant stage to the childhood stage to the adolescent stage to the young adult stage to the mature adult stage to the senior citizen stage and to the blessed golden years, if they remain that long. Every stage marks a transition and movement from one phase to another.

Societies change, moving in a historical continuum that can never be reversed. Nations move in a unidirectional continuum always marching with the course of time, and each writing its own history. No society lives unto itself. All come under the influence of other societies, and both influence others and are influenced by others. There is no tribe or individual which does not fit into this relationship, to a greater or lesser extent. Even the jet airplane that flies over the jungle tribesman causes the tribesman to respond with awe, wonder, fear, or worship.

Every missionary who sets his foot on foreign soil is an agent of change, as well as every government official, army soldier, or explorer. All sociologists and anthropologists know that change is inevitable. It comes from human influence and from nonhuman sources. Changes in weather and climatic conditions cause response. People movements cause changes in other peoples. Social changes cause a chain reaction with far-reaching results.

Missionaries are falsely accused of destroying culture. Their actions, life style, and teaching do cause changes. Missionaries are agents of change, and that by design. Instead of destroying culture, missionaries direct culture by bringing the individual and society a sense of worth and well-being.

Change is inevitable. The question is: "How fast will change come, in what direction will it go, and what form will it take?" To equate change with destruction is erroneous. To equate the missionary with destruction is diabolic.

Missionaries are professional agents of change. They are not intent on changing culture, but they seek primarily a spiritual change. That change influences all areas of life of the individual and society. Moral change immediately follows spiritual change. Then a multitude of social relationships, economic practices, and cultural patterns find themselves influenced by the initial movement. Conversion itself means a turning around. New thoughts produce new life patterns. When conversion takes place, change is bound to occur. As Paul stated it, "Therefore if any man is in Christ, *he* is a new creature; the old things passed away; behold, new things have come" (2 Cor. 5:17).

Conversion includes turning from old ways and norms to new norms and life patterns. It produces a new goal as well as a new set of values. It produces a new world view. It produces a transformation which effects every sphere of one's life and being.

The missionary is not one who sets out to change cultures. He seeks to change the heart. He knows that as a man "thinks within himself, so he is" (Prov. 23:7). Thus the anthropologist and the sociologist should be the most intimately related with the missionary in his enterprise. The problem comes when the anthropologist, sociologist, and missionary have a different world view. Naturally an evolutionary world view and a theistic world view are conflicting. The reality of the conflict is in the theological sphere, not in the anthropological. But the consequences of the difference spill over into the anthropological and sociological areas and consequently influence decisions. An understanding of the nature of this conflict will encourage the missionary to pursue, without apology or deviation, his defined goal—that of seeking the conversion of the lost.

Understanding the universality of change also brings us to recognize the fact that all change takes place within a context. Even conversion is contextually related. (See chapter "The Conversion Process.") It is both the result of context and cause of new context.

Readiness for Change

Several elements of a culture demonstrate readiness for, degree of, and direction of change. The missionary does well to consider these signs.

First, *dissatisfaction* presents a context that is ready for change. Political dissatisfaction demonstrates readiness for political change. Communism is most adept at taking advantage of a politically agitated situation. It may even move to try to produce the unrest that initiates the process by causing dissatisfaction to set the stage for overthrow.

When people become socially dissatisfied they begin to seek new social orders or relationships. Materialism thrives in an environment where the seed of dissatisfaction has been sown. Much of our present advertising is based on the premise that a man will buy a new car, television, or living room suite if he can be made to feel dissatisfied with his old.

Economic dissatisfaction produces a context for change. When people are dissatisfied with living conditions they will seek new patterns. People who live in a slash-and-burn context know the pattern of planting as long as the soil produces. They move on to other virgin soil when they are dissatisfied with the yield of the old field. Migrant cattle herders move with the available pasture, but when pasture runs out they will adapt to a farming life. Rural peoples, when dissatisfied with the economic life, will migrate to cities to try to find a more acceptable life-pattern. Failure to attain that only produces frustration and negative changes on the whole socioeconomic system.

Dissatisfaction with the whole lifestyle of affluence of our

W A S P (White, Anglo-Saxon, Protestant) society turned the youth to a grubbies and back to nature lifestyle. When the people of Israel became dissatisfied with the way they felt Jehovah was treating them, insisting that they be different from other peoples, they rebelled and turned after the ways and gods of the surrounding nations.

Dissatisfaction in any realm produces a context in which people are ready for change in that realm.

A second element which indicates people are ready for change is *disuse* of some cultural form. As long as a form has meaning it is adhered to readily. When a form loses meaning it may be continued just as a form, but sooner or later it will be altered or dropped. If there is no reason for dropping it, the custom may be continued simply as an element of tradition. Holidays are often examples of the disuse aspect. The Fourth of July celebration, and Thanksgiving Day, have to a great degree lost their significance. These holidays are traditional, and conveniently provide a free day that all enjoy, and so they are continued. Very few people go to church now on Thanksgiving Day to express their thanks to God, but the football stadiums are filled. A cultural substitution has taken place, following the disuse of a celebration. It was not a radical change, nor a total change. Rather it came slowly.

The church bell has fallen into disuse. In the days before rapid transportation the church bell would toll one hour before service time to alert the community that it was time to come to church. Then again at the hour of service it would signal time to begin. Now with people traveling much further, and everyone owning timepieces, the need for the church bell has disappeared. Today most churches do not have a church bell. A few have substituted organ chimes for the bell, performing a different function. Formerly factory whistles signaled work shift changes. Now that is falling into disuse. Of course the horse and buggy have fallen into disuse, being replaced by the automobile.

In many communities the clay jug has given way to the pipe for carrying water to the home. The pipe serves the function of the water pot, and the pot has become an artifact in the museum. With the change, the social time when women meet daily at a given time and place for social exchange, as well as exchange of news, has been destroyed.

Likewise, religious practices may fall into disuse. When they no longer have meaning they can be readily dropped, or some substitute invoked in their place. Usually, however, religious practices are not dropped until a functional substitute is introduced.

A third element signifying readiness for change is the *deprivation* of some functional element. Cattle herders that are deprived of their pasture are forced to change. They either migrate to new pastures, or turn to other life styles. Some may turn to farming, or to industry, or to begging. The American Indian, suddenly deprived of his hunting grounds, and thus of his source of life, suffered irreparable damage. When the man's provider role was removed, the society became a matriarchal society, and the man turned to drink.

If the U.S. becomes totally, or even significantly, deprived of its oil, dramatic changes will take place. Recognizing the potential reality has stirred many Americans.

Usually a people deprived of a commodity will search for a substitute. In place of oil coal, alcohol, and atomic energy are being sought as substitutes. Houses are being equipped with solar heating. Changes in building patterns will be inevitable. Houses may become smaller, and living conditions adjusted.

On the other side *appeal* of some desired or perceived attraction presents a context calling for change. Appeal may come from social, moral, spiritual, political, or economic sources. Whatever the source, the appeal will govern the action. The stronger the appeal, the stronger the action. Thus we ask the question, "Is the appeal of Christ strong enough to break the bonds of tradition, and family, and custom?"

The Process of Change

The process of change may come in one of four ways: substitution, borrowing, accommodation, innovation.

Substitution

Substitution is that process whereby one entity of culture may be substituted for something new. A toothbrush may be substituted for chewing a fibrous twig to clean the teeth. No drastic change is evident. One type of clothing may be substituted for another. Most of the world today recognizes the Western style dress as a status symbol, though certain areas retain their own in demonstration of national identity.

Automobiles are substituted for ox carts and horses wherever they are affordable. Tractors for plowing and farm usage are substituted for oxen, horses, and the hand hoe wherever the economy permits. With the substitution of one element many others are affected.

Borrowing

Borrowing is that process of change whereby one people or group see in another group something that is desirable. They say in actuality, "We like that" and proceed to adopt the custom, or the entity whatever it may be. Tribesmen may borrow canoe building from a neighboring tribe. They may borrow fishing nets from a more distant people. People may borrow a material thing such as a German camera and build an industry on camera manufacture, or an English car and build an industry of automobile manufacture. A people may borrow a school system, and adopt the English school system such as in India and in Nigeria. A people may borrow a system of worship, and follow a Roman Catholic pattern, or an Anglican pattern, or a Plymouth Brethren pattern.

Borrowing can occur in any realm of life, and one must recognize the possibility of a people borrowing Christianity simply because it appeals, without understanding its nature.

Accommodation

Accommodation (or adaptation) also produces changes. Substituting a gasoline motor for a horse in front of a carriage produced an adaptation that has today produced the multi-horse powered vehicle that races over our interstate highways.

Had there been no such adaptation of the first vehicle there would have been no interstate system today. Family life would have undoubtedly remained much more closely related. Thus the rapid transit, result of adaptation, has caused serious changes in the whole lifestyle and social system of our country.

Perhaps hospitals are one of the greatest and most influential examples of worldwide accommodation. Few countries knew of hospitals or health care until they were introduced by missionaries. Likewise schools have been adapted to almost every country, and have produced dramatic changes.

Adaptation of scriptural practice is today a prominent issue, known as contextualization, and related to the problem of syncretism. Syncretism and contextualization fall into the arena of adaptation. Syncretism is the amalgamation of *content* or practice that is unacceptable. Contextualization is the adaptation of *form* that might be acceptable within the Christian body.

When God ordered the children of Israel to enter the Promised Land, He forbade their accepting the foreign gods and all practices related to them. Syncretism was prohibted. Worship patterns and relics that were related to worship of false gods were to be entirely destroyed. Total separation was demanded. God commanded Moses:

> Speak to the sons of Israel and say to them, "When you cross over the Jordan into the land of Canaan, then you shall drive out all the inhabitants of the land from before you, and destroy all their *figured stones,* and destroy all their molten images and demolish all their high places; and you shall take possession of the land and live in it, for I have given the land to you to possess it." (Num. 33:51-53).

Contextualization is understood as dealing with form rather than content, and is approached as an element of communication. Prayer is one example of contextualization adaptation. Scripture is not specific in its instruction concerning the manner of prayer. Examples can be given of lifting up the hands, standing, or kneeling. All are acceptable in Scripture.

It would therefore seem to be acceptable to recognize any given pattern or posture for prayer as appropriate for believers provided they feel comfortable with it. Scripture is not specific about form, and adaptation of form to local pattern would seem to be in order. (See Chapter 2).

Care and discretion between syncretism and contextualization to determine lines of acceptability and norms for delineation are necessary.

Innovation

Innovation (or invention) is the fourth major element that produces change. Our own country's history, along with that of Europe, is a history of inventions. Electricity, the steam engine, gasoline engine, jet engine, telephone, telegraph, radio, television, are all producing dramatic changes that affect our way of life, material and social norms, and influence our moral judgments. Innovations in the electronic field have influenced our music. That, in turn, has its influence on the emotions of people of all ages. Dissatisfaction with materialism coupled with a hypocritical image of religion has caused many young people to turn to drugs, so that our country now has a drug culture which is fast becoming a socially acceptable lifestyle.

Agent of Change

The primary task of the missionary is to introduce Christ, not cultural change. Cultural and sociological changes will inevitably come as the result of the new life in Christ, but the missionary's respect for the existing norms and life patterns will go a long way in making him an acceptable individual. Anyone who attacks the existing pattern is sure to be rejected as a destroyer. By demonstrating his appreciation for and understanding of the old, the missionary demonstrates his right to be heard or followed as he presents his new message.

Thus, a missionary, to be an effective agent of change, must demonstrate his understanding of the old religion, moral practices, life pattern, and accepted norms. He does not tread on these, or he becomes a reject. Disrespect displayed to idols, or to accepted norms and standards of a people implies disrespect to the people who hold to these norms and worship those idols. Consider Paul in Athens. He did not display disrespect for the idols nor for the Athenians. To have shown disrespect of the idols would have displayed disrespect of the people. Instead he presented a more excellent way.

A missionary, as an agent of change and introducer of new truth, must first of all operate through individuals. Individuals of the target group become bridges through whom a new message and a new life pattern are introduced. The missionary then seeks to gain acceptance, confidence, friendship, respect, and leadership recognition within the context of the target group perception. The self-image of a people cannot be attacked or destroyed if the missionary is to gain acceptance, identification, and rapport. Self-respect is a vital part of relationship-building and must be maintained. Even recognition of one's own self as a sinner does not destroy the recognition of the worth of one's self as man. When the missionary attains the position of recognized leadership by an individual or group then the individual or group is ready to accept his witness and leadership. Then and only then will he influence individuals to become innovators within their own people-group. New converts are the innovators of the new message, life, and community within the target group. They are the ones who dare to believe differently, think differently, and act differently. The first converts establish the image of the church introduced into any given society. They are both the agents and pattern formers of the new body of followers of Christ within their culture.

Areas of Change

Finally, a missionary must give some consideration to the areas of change desired. The change will be introduced through the new converts. They become the innovators of a new life pattern and the prototype of the new church. As the church becomes better there is less and less novelty in it, simply because image has already been established. However, every local group of believers does establish certain patterns as norms within the society. The basic question that the missionary faces is, "What areas of culture and social mores must change?" Certainly murder, sacrifices to idols, stealing other men's wives or adultery, must be recognized as intolerable within any Christian community anywhere in the world. Scripture gives clear guidance in these areas. They are areas affecting society in moral and ethical matters. At the other extreme, hair styles, type of dress, occupational endeavors, food, and eating habits are largely amoral and unrelated to ethical standards, just as housing and economic level are usually not related to moral issues.

Frequently we find the consideration of legitimacy of practices presented as a continuum (Figure 43). Perhaps a study of Scripture would lead to fewer issues in the questionable area. Certainly Scripture is quite clear in the whole area of morals and moral actions. Scripture does not make moral decisions based on cultural norms or acceptance or rejection. Scripture in no way allows each culture to define sin, as some would lead us to believe. That which is sin in one culture is sin in all cultures. It is not right for one culture to practice infanticide, and wrong for another. It is not right for one culture to practice polygamy, and wrong for another. Either it is right for all or wrong for all. Scripture, as the revelation of God to all men, cannot be interpreted as having or allowing different standards for various cultures.

Likewise the church, in all cultures, has the same guide for deciding moral, ethical, and spiritual issues, and for estab-

Figure 43
The Legitimacy of Practices

Moral Issues	Questionable Issues	Nonmoral Issues
Taboos Prohibitions	Doubts	Customary Norms Life Patterns

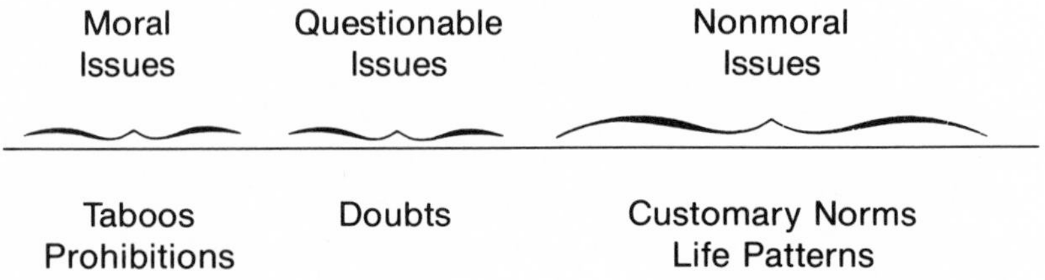

lishing norms. Does this then mean that what we have decided in the West is the norm? Definitely not. It simply means that together the missionary and the national convert must go carefully to the Scripture to discern what the scriptural norm must be, and be ready to apply it bidirectionally. It may call for a new evaluation of taboos, and prohibitions may have to be reexamined. It certainly means that many aspects of culture and social practice will be recognized as completely beyond the judgment of Scripture. Where Scripture does not address itself either in precept or principle, directly or indirectly, the missionary can certainly refrain from trying to introduce any change. He is not primarily an agent of cultural change. But where Scripture addresses itself directly, the missionary then has the obligation to teach. The target group must understand that "The Scripture teaches," not "The missionary teaches." The reason for, and the effect of, change thus introduced must be understood.

Are there norms that the church must establish for the new body and believer? Undoubtedly. But they must be scripturally expressed. No man needs to be taken out of his culture to become a Christian. But all cultures will be influenced by a body of believers within that culture. The matter of cultural adjustment to the understanding of Scripture can be illustrated by a circle (Figure 44).

Figure 44
Cultural Adjustments and Scriptural Understanding

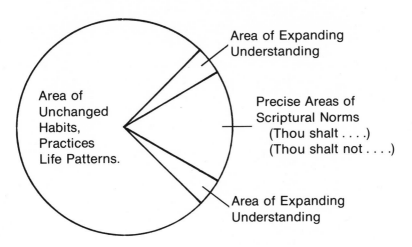

When an individual turns to Christ, he will understand certain areas of precise Scriptural norms. There will be areas of expanding understanding and adjustment, but the greater area of normal life pattern will remain unchanged. The scriptural truths will slowly penetrate into every area of man's thinking, even as sin crept into and influenced every area of his life previously. But change and accomodation come slowly and deliberately. They require the ingredient of time.

Bibliography

Arensberg, Conrad M., and Niehoff, Arthur H. *Introducing Social Change: A Manual for Community Development.* Chicago: Aldine Publishing, 1967.

Barnett, Homar G. *Innovations: The Basis of Cultural Change.* New York: McGraw-Hill, 1963.

Bascom, W. R., and Herskovits, M. J., eds. *Continuity and Change in African Cultures.* Chicago: University of Chicago Press, 1958.

Gluckman, Max. *Customs and Conflict in Africa.* New York: Barnes and Noble, 1969.

Herskovits, Melville J. *Acculturation: The Study of Culture Contact.* Magnolia, MA: Peter Smith Publishers, 1958.

Hesselgrave, David J. *Communicating Christ Cross-Culturally.* Grand Rapids, Zondervan, 1978.

Keesing, Felix M. *Culture Change: An Analysis and Bibliography of Anthropological Sources to 1952.* New York: Octagon Books, 1973.

Kluckhohn, Clyde. *Mirror For Man: A Survey of Human Behavior and Social Attitudes.* New York: Fawcett Publications, 1957.

Luzbetak, Louis J. *The Church and Cultures: An Applied Anthropology for the Religious Worker.* Pasadena, CA: William Carey Library Publishers, 1976.

Malinowski, Bronislaw. *The Dynamics of Culture Change.* Ed. Phyllis M. Kaberry. 1961. Reprint. Westport, CT: Greenwood Press, 1976.

Mead, Margaret, ed. *Cultural Patterns and Technical Change.* New York: New American Library, Mentor Books, 1955.

Rogers, Everett M. *Diffusion of Innovations.* New York: Free Press of Glencoe, 1962.

———and Shoemaker, F. Floyd. *Communication of Innovations.* 2d ed. New York: Free Press, 1971.

Tippett, Alan R. *Solomon Islands Christianity: A Study of Growth and Obstruction.* Pasadena, CA: William Carey Library Publishers, 1975.

11

Receptivity

Closely related to the study of change and accommodation is the study of receptivity, or responsiveness to the gospel. No one will deny that in some areas the people seem prepared for the gospel, and when a missionary enters there is an immediate following. In other areas missionaries report that they have labored faithfully for many years and seen almost no fruit. Yet they persist in their faithful witness.

No attempt will be made to discredit any missionary endeavor, nor are there any judgmental implications against the individuals who do not have success stories to report. Our study is directed toward the issue of responsiveness or non-responsiveness, receptivity or rejection, and the factors that contribute to the attitude of the individuals or groups concerned.

Initially *historical factors* may be considered. The Islamic world and the Christian world have had sociological conflict for centuries. The conflict of power, with the history of the Crusades, has undoubtedly created strong tension resulting in a Muslim's deep-seated rejection of Christianity. The animosity has been further developed by the teaching of the religious leaders of Islam against Christianity, planting hatred toward Christianity in the minds of the followers of Islam. Christianity and Islam are by their nature antithetical.

If one does not sense some degree of dissatisfaction with his existing state he is not ready to look for change. Islam, a religion of works gives a sense of accomplishment and satisfaction to the follower so that he does not sense a need for any change.

Responsiveness to the gospel cannot be separated from the *sociological* and *cultural* aspects of some degree of dissatisfaction. Sociological dissatisfaction may cause a desire for sociological change. If the sociological position is related to a religious belief, then the religious belief may be questioned in search of a new sociological status. This is the condition in India. The sociological structure of a caste system is largely the result of a Hindu religion and sociological system. Both are intertwined. The people who are at the top of the pyramid have little to gain and much to lose by a change. They feel no need for change. They are the most unresponsive to the gospel, as the history of missions has proven. Most mission approaches in India were made first to the Brahman peoples, thinking that if the upper caste could be won, then the message would penetrate downward through the society. However, time has shown that there was very little response among the upper–caste people. They had everything to lose and nothing to gain sociologically.

On the contrary, it was discovered that when the gospel was presented to the outcastes who were dissatisfied with their state in life there was then more acceptance. As part of the message the individuals were given a sense of self-recognition and self-worth. The gospel provided the answer to a felt need. Those individuals had everything to gain and nothing to lose sociologically by the change.

Anthropologically speaking, whenever an advocate of change and a situation which is ripe for change converge, some reaction is bound to occur. This response will fall into one of the following categories: 1) Total rejection, 2) Acceptance with modification, 3) Total acceptance. The modification may include substitution in form or in function. Receptive populations, people ready for change, will be the most ready for total acceptance. Peoples who have gone through some recent upheaval and just reached a new steady-state will be the most unreceptive.

Anthony Wallace has presented the movements of society

Figure 45

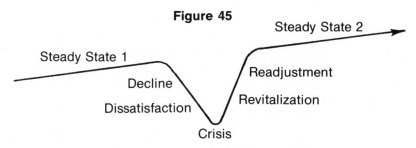

in a five-step pattern in his "Revitalization Movements." (See Figure 45.) He shows that all cultures move from steady-state to steady-state. They progress from one period of relatively fixed-state to another period of relatively fixed-state, but that the new fixed-state is arrived at by passing through crisis times. There is first decline of the old, producing dissatisfaction. Then a crisis moment or event which gives rise to a new position. Then a tapering off in the new steady-state.[1]

When a people are in the decline and dissatisfaction state they are looking for some phenomenon that will satisfy the felt need and produce the desired change. Moses was that God-appointed leader for the people of Israel who entered into a historic period to lead the people of God out into a new life. Since murmuring had become a part of their life-habit during the dissatisfaction stage there is no wonder that some murmuring carried into the revitalization stage.

When a people have just gone through a readjustment period and reached a new steady-state they are at the point of highest resistance to further change. They have experienced traumatic changes and are just in the position of finding themselves confident after chaos or confusion. The last thing they want is further confusion. At this point people say "Leave me alone, let me settle down."

The present movement among the Maguzawa people of northern Nigeria is an example of the combination of historical, sociological, and anthropological factors combining to produce a people ready for change, and receptive to the gospel.

1. Anthony F. C. Wallace, "Revitalization Movements," *American Anthropologist*, 58 (1956): 264-281.

The name *Maguzawa* means The Runner. It is used of the people who rejected the invasion of the Islamic forces into their territory years ago. They were tribespeople who had an animistic, paganistic religion. They defied the Islamic peoples who tried to enter their territory and take over their land. Rather than submit to Islamic rule and religion, these tribes people ran from the invaders. Through the course of time the Islamic powers set up governmental control over the central cities and major villages, and the Maguzawa were outcasts to the society. The ruling class were known as God-worshipers and the Maguzawa were pagans.

A deep resentment grew between the two. Children of the God-worshipers were not allowed to play with the children of the pagans. The Maguzawa were outcasts of society, and consequently developed a lifestyle of their own. They became farmers of small plots surrounding the villages and lived in their own compounds in extended family units. Marriage was limited to marriage to other Maguzawa families.

Recently the government of Nigeria has adopted a policy of required elementary education for all children of the country. Part of that educational program includes religious knowledge. All parents are asked whether they prefer Islamic teaching of the Koran or Christian teaching of the Bible. Either is an open option and free choice is guaranteed. Because of the historical setting, and sociological treatment these people have received under Islamic control, the Maguzawa have almost totally opted to take the Bible knowledge courses as the program for their children.

The Maguzawa also know that the health clinics and rural development programs are favorable to them. These programs are aligned with Christianity in their minds. Thus the image of Christianity has done much to make it the most desirable option. Today no one wants to be a pagan. The term has a most unacceptable connotation. It carries the thought of *uncivility*, and the government of Nigeria is moving strongly to make the country a leader in the African continent. It has perhaps the most, by way of natural resources, and the highest population of the continent. It is a developing country and its people are moving into leadership roles. Paganism and incivility do not go along with development and leadership.

Consequently the Maguzawa, when confronted with the option, finds himself sociologically dissatisfied with his present state, culturally moving to new life patterns, and historically conditioned to choose Christianity as his most viable and attractive alternative. As a result the Evangelical Church of West Africa has found itself with a ripe harvest field into which it is sending its field evangelists to reap the harvest while it is ripe. Until these recent changes began to influence the Maguzawa people there seemed to be no response to the gospel. People were content to live worshiping the household god that their father had set up, and in fear of the evil spirits that constantly taunted them. Today there is a turning to Christ that is so fast that the church cannot keep up with the baptism of new believers. Here is a receptive people who have become so through recognizable influences.

There is no doubt but that many of the homogeneous units that are presented as case studies who are found to be responsive at a given point in history have similar historical, sociological, and cultural factors that have prepared them to be a responsive people. This is in accord with the working of the Spirit of God in His way at His time with the people of His choosing. If we consider ourselves to be "coworkers together with God" then we have no problem of moving with Him into a field that is ripe for harvest.

Varying responsiveness of different groups of people at different times is an observable fact. It is observable in the Bible. The common people were more responsive than the Pharisees. The poor were more responsive than the rich. The Galileans were apparently more responsive than the Judeans. Among the Gentiles in general there were those who were known as God-fearers who were especially prepared to respond when the gospel was enunciated. The Bereans were more responsive than the nearby Thessalonians (Acts 17).

Varying responsiveness is observable historically among different groups, and at different points of time. The Aymara of the Quechua tribe demonstrate a movement at a given point of time. For years there was no apparent responsiveness, and then in the early 1970s a movement of the Spirit of God seemed to come over the whole nation. Our own national history witnesses to the "revival" movements which are a parallel to the phenomena.[2]

Varying responsiveness is also observable from country to country, though there is seldom whole country responsiveness at one time. Burma is 3.3 percent professing Christian, while neighboring Thailand is only 0.1 percent. However, most of the response in Burma has been among the Karen and Kachin tribespeople. Other groups have not so responded. Ninety percent of all of India's professing Christians are in the Kerala, Assam, and Nagaland regions. Chile has recently seen an explosion of Pentecostal Church growth, so that 10 percent of the population are now professing Protestants.

Responsiveness in relation to cultural change may be influenced by several factors. Acculturation opens people up to innovations. Adaptation to new cultural patterns accelerates the willingness to accept the religious beliefs of those whose culture is being adopted. Thus immigrants become prime objects of acculturation and acceptance of the gospel that is related to the cultural adaptation.

People in new settlements are generally more responsive. Insecurity and break from the old contribute to the preparation for acceptance of something new. Uprooted and immigrant peoples fall into this classification. Rural peoples who move into the big cities find themselves with insecurity in the new environment and often frustrated. Break from the old has transpired. Insecurity however also produces uncertainty about hastily accepting anything new, and most peoples do not readily accept the offer without carefully weighing its consequences. Their acceptance will be with great caution and trepidation. They want—but they are not certain.

Nationalism may provide a context either for or against responsiveness. In Korea the church became a rallying point for opposition to the Japanese. Response to Christianity became

2. See J. Edwin Orr as the historian on these events.

a source of security and strength. Thus about 40 percent of the military became professing Christians by the end of the war. A need was felt, the army had many witnesses in the persons of the U. S. army chaplains, and response was evident.

Freedom from peer pressure and family pressure also contribute to a responsive environment. In a tightly knit society the matter of individual choice is greatly reduced. Tribe, family, and peer action is determined by fixed rules. People operate within that mentality and context. In such societies personal choice is almost annihilated. Until the community changes, no individual is free to choose his own way. The missionary who does not understand that context will labor to attract only the renegade of his society, and may inadvertently be presenting the image of Christianity as being the destroyer of the home, and of society.

Spiritual responsiveness is closely allied with the recognition of unmet spiritual needs. New innovations may alert a people to the fact that their spiritual needs are not being satisfied by their present worship pattern. Idols may become recognized as only manmade images of stone or wood and without power. Liturgical forms, whether of sacrifices or other patterns, may be recognized as only superficial and a vacuum be perceived. Such would be a working of the Spirit of God to prepare a people for acceptance of the gospel. If the message of true redemption is not presented at that time the people will turn to some other religion and will then become resistant to the gospel. If they settle on one new form or belief they will resist any other change that would upset their newly established steady-state.

Response may come as a result of people seeking release from fear. Voodooism is a religion of great fear. Sacrifices are offered to appease the devil and evil spirits. People's hearts cry for release from fear, but that very fear keeps them from turning to Christ. They fear· what the spirits will do if they turn from their practices and worship. Response would be there: fear keeps them from responding.

Response may come because people need a sense of self-worth, or new goals, or a rallying point, perhaps against humiliating oppression. When Christ is presented as the One who can provide an answer to these felt needs, and there is demonstration of His power and plan, people will respond to the offer.

Responsiveness is also vitally connected to the *communication process*. In many places the rejection is not of the message—it may be rejection of the communication and communicator. Some are seriously asking the question whether the U. S. missionary is the best communicator to go to the American Indian. The Navajo has a deep resentment against the U. S. missionary because of the history behind him. The white man took away his land and his livelihood. A missionary has a great obstacle to overcome. Would a missionary from the Quechua tribe of Bolivia be a more suitable communicator to the Navajo? Or perhaps one from Guatemala, or Mexico?

It is doubtful that an Indian from India would have much acceptance among the Pakistani peoples. There is a hatred built on historical factors. Would an Indonesian be a more acceptable channel to the Pakistani?

Responsiveness is enhanced by the effectiveness of the source. The messenger is more effective if he understands the receiver. He is more effective if he identifies himself with the recipient. He is more effective if he has a congenial personality that adapts itself to the personality trait of the recipient group. He is more effective if he can present the message in a way that relates itself to the felt needs of the people. God's man in God's place at God's time recognizes the distinctiveness of each individual and his place in God's sovereign pattern.

One serious question needs to be asked. Have the people truly rejected the message, or was the communication of the message not clear to them? If the communication was not clear then we have no right to say the message has been rejected. As those interested in a proclamation of the truth we must assume that the problem may have been with the communication and move to rectify that, rather than turning from anyone who may not have responded.

An understanding of receptivity and rejection patterns does not direct itself to the question of whether we engage in missionary endeavor or not to a people. It addresses itself to the questions of how and who, as well as where. Dr. George Peters has stated that in his study he has never found a responsive group where there has not been at least 30 years of contact with the gospel prior to the movement. If that be true it means an entire generation has had some contact to form an imagery of Christianity before the ready response came.

Varying responses to the gospel message should have a definite impact on the strategy employed. Seed sowing is a characteristic of pioneer missionary work, and of ministry among resistant peoples. Harvesting is the outcome that is anticipated. Where there is no seed sowing there will be little harvest. A harvest theology can never nullify either the command of the Lord to "Go, and make disciples of all nations" or the practical reality that a harvest demands a prior sowing. Paul's declaration to the Corinthians stands: "I planted the seed, Apollos watered it, but God made it grow" (1 Cor. 3:6 NIV).

One of the most common passages referred to in considering the Biblical teaching on the subject of receptivity is the parable of the sower, Luke 8:4-8. The interpretation demands reflection in two areas: first, the *context* in which it was spoken; second, Christ's own *interpretation* given to the diciples in vss. 9-15.

The context

Jesus had gone to Nazareth, his home town, and taught in the synagogue. There He was rejected and spurned. Nazareth was not ready for the message He had come to proclaim, partly because He was a home–town boy (Luke 4:14-28). From there He went to Capernaum, in Galilee, and taught and performed miracles. In Galilee He was well received (Luke 4:31-41). He continued in the region of Capernaum for some time, traveling into every village and town of the region. As He was traveling, He was sowing the seed equally upon all, ministering and healing in every place. Then, one special day the time came for the instruction of the parable. People from every town and village had gathered to see what He would do that day. It must have been quite a crowd if the account of the feeding of the five thousand recorded in chapter 9 is any indication.

The interpretation

Christ is addressing Himself to those who were present. The seed to which He referred was the Word of God which He had sown equally upon all alike. Every town to which He had gone and from which the people had come out had received an equal distribution of the seed. However, there was a difference in the soil upon which the seed had fallen. The people of some towns were like the hard–packed pathway. When the seed fell there it did not penetrate at all. It lay on top of the soil and was soon picked up by Satan and taken away, so the people would not believe and be saved. The Word was gone from them. In other villages the people were like rock, so that when the seed fell upon them there was no moisture in the rock, or depth in the soil to cause the seed to grow, so it died. Other villages were composed of those hearers who received the Word, but who had so many entangling alliances with the world, and with riches and possessions, that the material cares choked out the spiritual truth and it soon succumbed. Finally, among some of the people and towns there were those who were prepared for the Word when it came. Among those the seed found reception. It fell into good ground. It was watered and nourished and grew and produced fruit.

Christ proclaimed that the seed was the same. It was sown equally upon all. The difference was in the recipients, and the recipients would bear the responsibility for what they did with the seed. So He says to the people to whom He was speaking: "He who has ears to hear, let him hear" (Luke 8:8).

There is no question but that Christ is speaking in terms of seed sowing, and the responsibility of the hearer. In that vein He instructed His disciples, as He sent them out: "Take nothing for the journey. . . . Whatever house you enter, stay there until you leave that town. If people do not welcome you, shake the dust off your feet when you leave their town, as a testimony against them" (Luke 9:3-5 NIV).

Degrees of receptivity among peoples is a real phenonenon that the missionary endeavor faces. Because of that it takes a task force to do the job. There are differing gifts of the Spirit for different ministries. Some missionaries are seed-sowers, who labor in soil preparation and faithful ministry through long, tedious years. Others come upon a harvest field ripe to harvest. They call for other laborers to "Come, help us gather the harvest before it is too late."

At the judgment all will be rewarded equally, those who labored long and hard and those who reaped the harvest finally. But let each be convinced of his own place, according to his talent and gift, in accordance with God's direction to Him, and be aware of his particular contribution.

Bibliography

Barnett, Homer G. *Innovations: The Basis of Cultural Change.* New York: McGraw-Hill, 1963.

Herskovits, Melville J. *Cultural Dynamics.* New York: Alfred A. Knopf, 1964.

Liao, David C. E. *The Unresponsive: Resistant or Neglected?* Pasadena, CA: William Carey Library Publishers, 1979.

McGavran, Donald A., ed. *Church Growth and Christian Mission.* Pasadena, CA: William Carey Library Publishers, 1976.

_____*Understanding Church Growth.* Rev. ed. Grand Rapids: Eerdmans, 1980.

Manners, Robert A., ed. *Process and Pattern in Culture.* Chicago: Aldine Publishing, 1964.

Nida, Eugene A. *Message and Mission: The Communication of the Christian Faith.* Pasadena, CA: William Carey Library Publishers, 1975.

Pentecost, Edward C. *Reaching the Unreached.* Pasadena, CA: William Carey Library Publishers, 1974.

Pickett, J. W., et al. *Church Growth and Group Conversion.* Pasadena, CA: William Carey Library Publishers, 1973.

Redfield, Robert. *A Village That Chose Progress: Chan Kom Revisited.* Chicago: University of Chicago Press, 1962.

Rogers, Everett M. *Diffusion of Innovations.* New York: Free Press of Glencoe, 1962.

Tippett, Alan R. *Church Growth and the Word of God.* Grand Rapids: Eerdmans, 1970.

_____ed. *God, Man, and Church Growth.* Grand Rapids: Eerdmans, 1973.

_____*Verdict Theology in Missionary Theory.* Pasadena, CA: William Carey Library Publishers, 1973.

Wallace, Anthony F. C., "Revitalization Movements." *American Anthropologist,* 58 (1956): 264-281.

12

The Homogeneous-Unit Principle

God has from creation operated in an orderly pattern working through special group dynamics. He created the heavens and the earth, making a special significant distinction between the two. They were different in nature, even though like in substance, made out of the same chemical material.

In the days of creation God made light and darkness. The light He called day and the darkness He called night. There is a particularism to each, with an unmistakable difference. Then came the division of waters above and waters beneath, followed by a division of the waters below from the earth below, so there were seas and dry land, both part of the earth. Again the act of God in creation produced vegetation and seed, each plant producing its own seed, and a particularism was established. Then came the creation of animals, each after its kind.

We are not told when the angelic beings were created, but the fact that they were created is certain. They constitute a very particular body, with a special relationship to God, and constitute the first body of beings of God's creation.

Finally God moved to create man, distinct from all of the previous creation, and distinct from the angelic beings. And within the realm of man there were two: Adam and Eve—both created in the image of God, with their own identity and distinction, according to the particular purpose of His will for each. It would seem then that particularism is a part of God's plan and operation from all eternity.

In the first period of world history we understand that there was only one people, and one family, the family of Adam. There was one language, one race, one ethnic people. But the time of that generation was limited. Sin entered and afflicted all of the descendants of Adam and Eve. Yet from among the multitudes of the great-grandchildren of Adam and Eve, God chose one family through whom He would replenish the earth, after bringing a deluge to destroy all flesh that was upon the face of the earth.

The deluge came and went. Noah and his family replenished the earth with inhabitants, but the new generation of mankind was no different from the earlier generation. Sin was present. God did not choose to destroy the new generation. Rather He chose to offer a plan of redemption to all. The nature of that plan must be considered elsewhere as a study of theology. But here the relevant factor is that, dealing with mankind with a redemptive purpose rather than with immediate judgment, God chose to disperse mankind over all the earth and did so by initiating language change, cultural change, and family or ethnic change. At Babel (Gen. 11) we find the beginning of ethnolinguistic groups, dispersed into different geographic and thus physical situations, from which all ethnic, linguistic, tribal, and racial groups emerged.

The process of change for some must have been very rapid. For others it may have been more delayed. The fact is that out of that beginning, of one family of humanity, or one ethnic unit—subdivided initially into three family units, the sons of Ham, Shem, and Japheth—many families were initiated, with linguistic and cultural differences being formed. All were equally man made in the image of God. All were of equal worth, but distinctives marked groups as never before.

Here we have the beginning of homogeneous units, people who formed themselves into distinct groups, recognizing a distinctiveness that identified them. Each had a sense of belonging to his own group with whom he could communicate and identify. Each knew his relationship with others of his own group, and identified himself with his own.

From Genesis 11 to Genesis 12 a long period of history is passed over with only a review of the generations. We are to understand, however, that through that period people groups grew into nations. We know that by this time the nations of Chaldea, Egypt, Assyria, and Canaan had developed. Just what their numbers were we do not know, but they were nations in their own eyes, with their kings, rulers, social systems, and recognizable distinctives. Their homogeneity was identifiable.

Abraham, a particularly chosen individual was singled out from among all the nations, and from among all the families, to perform a special function for God. In Abraham God purposed to begin His program of a special nature through whom a new homogeneous unit would be formed. It was the family of Abraham which became the Hebrew people with identifiable Hebrew characteristics. In due time this brought many consequences, with the well-recognized distinction between sons of Abraham, the chosen people of God, and the "non-sons" or Gentiles.

Our purpose is not to trace the redemptive line through Abraham, Moses, and David, to Christ, but to recognize the fact that God has always recognized identifiable units of people, seeing and knowing them, and loving them as His creatures.

Today the world population has increased dramatically. At the time of Christ the world population was approximately one fourth of one billion. Today it has surpassed the four billion mark, and all the members of humanity exist in some relationship with others who form group units. Language, parentage, and sociological factors all delineate the individuals into marked and recognized entities. These are homogeneous units. The concept is as old as Babel. The reality is before us.

During the time of the rise of Israel to nationhood and its taking possession of the land promised to the descendants of Abraham, God dealt with Israel in a particularist way. Israel was the chosen ". . . possession among all the peoples, for all the earth is Mine; and you shall be to Me a kingdom of priests and a holy nation" (Exodus 19:5,6).

During the years following, Jehovah dealt with other nations in kindness or in judgment according to the way they treated His chosen people, while at the same time working through His people to be His witnesses to the other nations concerning Himself as the "One True and Living God."

God's pattern through the world's history has been to deal with nations as distinct entities of people. When the fulness of time came for the formation of the church there was one big question that had to be answered: Could peoples other than Jews become Christians and maintain their cultural identity, or did they have to become Jews to be Christians? This was the question that brought the apostles and elders together for the first church council meeting in Jerusalem (Acts 15). The decision was that followers of the Lord could maintain their own cultural heritage and identity and still be true members of the body of Christ. This was nothing less than the recognition of homogeneous units within the church. The church could be made up of distinct groups, each with his own identity, and all sharing identity with Christ.

Apparently, the first church council did not see this as a break in the unity for which Christ had prayed in His prayer recorded in John 17. And since Paul was there, apparently he saw no conflict with what he later wrote to the Ephesian church in Ephesians 4.

From the initiation of the church distinctives were recognized. These were not in degree, but in living circumstances. In each place where Paul went, he sowed the seed of the Word of God and a local church grew up. Each was a local church, with distinct identity, and all with the same Word and Spirit of the Lord within them. Each differed in local color, but all were the same in nature. Thus there was diversity within unity.

Today the homogeneous unit principle has taken on major proportions in the consideration of missiologists and church planters. It divides itself into three major emphases: 1. Homogeneous units as a communication factor; 2. Homogeneous units as an evangelistic factor; 3. Homogeneous units as local church entities.

Homogeneous Units as a Communication Factor

A homogeneous unit is a sociological body, sufficiently large and distinct to recognize itself as a unit. By the very nature of the unit it is a body that recognizes a linguistic pattern, a psychological mentality, and a cultural identity. These three elements are the very foundation elements of communication. (See chapter "The Communication Process.") It is therefore the most natural phenomenon to expect that communication will pass clearly among the group. When the conversion process is recognized as being a phenomenon that relates to all members of a group in a united society, it becomes even more clear that the communication process calls for mutual transmittal and response.

Only in the individualistic society of the West is a person expected to operate in a pattern as an individual. Only in the West does one have the liberty to act individualistically without being ostracized from his society. The homogeneous-unit concept and communication understanding are almost synonymous. For effective communication the common frame of reference is a vital perspective. Thus in the chapter on communication we used the two overlapping ovals as a representation (Figure 46).

Figure 46
Intracultural Communication

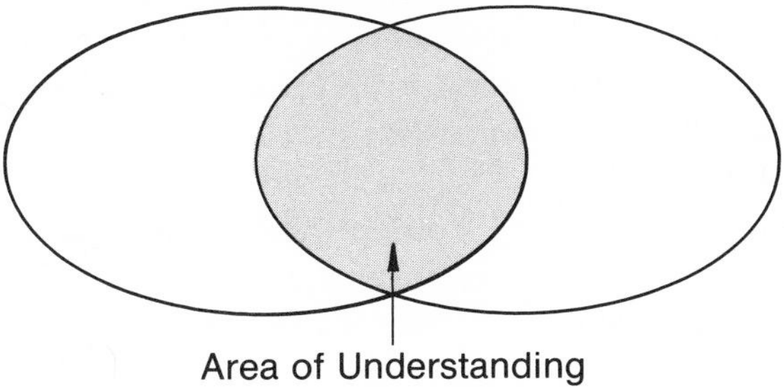

Area of Understanding

Within the homogeneous unit the two are almost congruous. Therefore, the level of communication and comprehension is high. It is therefore natural that in the communication of the gospel the interaction of a group of like mind, like culture, like language, will be the most fertile place for group comprehension and group response.

Such a communication approach may mean group rejection just as it may mean group acceptance. If a group, communicating among itself, decides to reject the message then the homogeneous-unit principle will dictate that there will be total rejection.

At this point we are driven to recognize that the work of the Holy Spirit is vital in the exercise of the will of the composite unit, and the missionary or communicator must observe the signs and be aware of the conditions. However, no group can be ruled out without adequately making the approach.

Understanding

The first essential in communication is to understand the position of the recipient. A presentation of the gospel must be made in terms of the felt need of the recipient group, that is to say, within his frame of reference. Announcement of a truth at an incomprehensible level is not attaining communication. The nature of communication demands speaking on the comprehension level of the individual or group. An understanding of the potential group becomes a vital factor in the preparatory work of the communicator.

Security

A second factor in the communication process is the security of the recipient. If the recipient senses that his security is being challenged, he is going to reject without giving consideration to the novelty. Sense of security and communication go hand-in-hand.

Where does security lie? In the relationship with the group. Thus from a communication viewpoint, if the communication is directed to and relevant to the group, security is not lost by group consideration. The individual within the group maintains his security by the assurance that he is within the framework of group action. His identity with the group gives him that support that he needs.

Communication to and within the homogeneous-unit is therefore a maintainer of the individual security.

Comprehension

Transmittal of a new concept can be accomplished only by a process of movement from the known to the unknown. Thus again we speak of one's frame of reference or world view. What does one know, and how does he view himself within his world? The homogeneous-unit principle suggests that a communicator can best communicate his message to others through an approach that takes into consideration the viewpoint and understanding of the recipient group. Making his message relevant to their understanding, culture, and social milieu, as well as linguistic patterns, adds to the degree of comprehension.

Every group has its own individuality which is to be taken into consideration in the communication and evangelization process. What is the religious belief of the target group? Discover it, and direct the application of the message to that aspect. Paul spoke to the Athenians concerning the unknown God for whom they had a place reserved. That approach was not used in Ephesus. Recognize that group dynamics is a communication factor.

A second aspect of comprehension is the insight into one's own idiosyncrasies. Until one recognizes the fact that he is part of a homogeneous unit himself, he is in danger of falling into the trap of thinking that he is a universalist and all are to be brought to his position and group perspective. There is truth which is absolute and universal; but communication of that truth is always linguistically and culturally oriented. Sensitivity to one's own linguistic, ethnic, cultural and historical environment adds to his effectiveness in being a cross-cultural communicator. Understanding of one's own environment adds appreciation for another's environment.

Homogeneous Units as an
Evangelism Factor

Recognizing security as a communication factor one can easily relate the same to evangelism. Effective evangelism is the product of effective communication. When the gospel is introduced to a group of like mind and interests there is a group response that either promotes or inhibits further communication and response. Through the communication process a group may be carried from a rejection position to a neutral position to a favorable or acceptance position.

Trying to evangelize a heterogeneous group may present group confusion. The communicator initially tries to amalgamate his audience into one solidified mindset in order to communicate effectively. Great mass-evangelism meetings have long introductory periods where singers and important individuals all work a psychological element into the molding of attitudes and of uniting the attenders into a group solidarity. In reality a new homogenity is being formed.

Approaching already existent homogeneous units is an effective means of presenting the gospel. It meets people where they are. It respects people as they are. It recognizes people for what they are. Evangelism of homogeneous units can be directed much more specifically to the group sentiment and needs, thus presenting more direct application.

Group response to evangelism also gives the immediate potential of a recognized church within the society. Individual evangelism within a group-oriented society often means only the renegades are won over. Thus through an individual approach to evangelism the image of the first church is that it is made up of social rejects, peripheral individuals, and is foreign to the society.

Often the process means a one-by-one growth, with great dependence on the missionary and possible ostracism from society. Group evangelism means there is strength in unity, with identification of the members to an in-group action. In such a situation both growth and influence are seen in the early stages of the local church development. Witness of the group becomes a vital factor.

Immediately following evangelism there is the normal response of group teaching. Thus the need of a church is early perceived. Leaders emerge from the disciples, and progress in the new life is noted.

Homogeneous Units as a Factor in Church Planting

As a result of group evangelism, group recognition of growth, leadership, and maturity emerge. Any group soon recognizes its own leadership. The Western process of electing leadership is only one way of choosing leaders.

Since part of any homogeneous-unit operation is the role or function of each member, the observable elements of a church can be recognized. The nonobservable spiritual elements can be detected only through manifest actions. Separation from sin, commitment to the Savior, growth in spiritual maturity, and demonstration of leadership will be related to observable criteria within the cultural pattern of the group.

Leadership patterns, recognition processes, and role responsibilities become vital factors in the formation of a local church. Scripture clearly outlines leadership characteristics, responsibilities, and functions. But the wise church planter will recognize that form adaptation is not only permissible, but appropriate for each homogeneous unit. Thus each local church establishes its own personal identity.

The planting of churches by homogeneous-unit affinity and operation is not only pragmatic, in that it has been proven to be effective, but it is natural. It follows observable phenomena, as normal operation pattern for man as man, who is by his very nature a being that operates within homogeneous norms.

Part of the importance of recognizing the homogeneous-unit local church is that the group has already learned to operate within the group pattern. The members are formed naturally into manageable groupings of society that are self-recognizing, friendly among themselves, operating within a recognized framework and structure. Those elements can be used in the formation of a church within that society. To insist in the formation of heterogeneous church units can introduce disquieting elements, causing sociological conflicts which may ultimately produce power conflicts in church operation as two or more entities seek a leadership role in the local church.

To talk about the ideal church may not be totally realistic in this present world of humanity. The homogeneous-unit church is a reality for a real world.

In considering the homogeneous-unit approach to evangelism and church planting one is faced with the question, "How do homogeneous-unit churches fit the Biblical pattern?" Or, "Is the homogeneous-unit church an end in itself?" The homogeneous-unit church is not an end in itself. Every local church is part of a universal church, made up of many local bodies. Each local body has its own recognizable identity, just as every member of a family has his or her own identity. No family member gives up his individuality in order to be part of a family. A white man, a black man, a yellow man can be part of one family of Christ without leaving his ethnic heritage to do so. Linguistic differences do not inhibit anyone from belonging to the universal body of Christ. This is the magnitude of the all-embracing love character of God that receives all men, just as they are, into one universal body without anyone having to leave any cultural norms—except sin, which has penetrated all and influences each one.

Within the universal church there are characteristics which will be recognized by every unit."But the fruit of the Spirit is love, joy, peace, patience, kindness, goodness, faithfulness, gentleness, self-control; against such things there is no law" (Gal. 5:22-23).

Every cultural group will respond to the absolute truth, and the manifestation will be mutually recognized, even though, perhaps, individually demonstrated. Every homogeneous-unit church will seek to extend itself and with that extend the universal church, but how it operates to extend itself will depend on its own potential and circumstances.

Growth in maturity will make acceptance of others from other homogeneous units a part of the life-pattern, so that seclusion is not a characteristic of the homogeneous unit. Spiritual growth will develop total respect for the differences of others rather than demanding that all become alike. Equality within diversity, and diversity within equality are more signs of spiritual maturity, than are demands for heterogeneity.

This is not to suggest in any way that diverse individuals and members of diverse societies cannot worship together. James' teaching is very much to the point. But James does not insist on amalgamation of diverse groups in order to worship. He is speaking of recognition of the individual and his rights.

India is one of the most difficult fields for solution of the homogeneous-unit church problem. Some propose that the homogeneous-unit approach is the most effective approach to church planting in that country, simply because of so many languages and social variations. Others proclaim that, because the government is trying to obliterate the caste system and has passed laws nullifying caste distinction, the church should be the first to demonstrate the fact that the body of Christ is one body, where "There is neither Jew nor Greek, there is neither slave nor free man, there is neither male nor female; for you are all one in Christ Jesus" (Gal. 3:28). But we need to remind ourselves that Paul was speaking of spiritual dimension, not physical. Christ never obliterated the sex difference between man and woman. Paul went on to give the interpretation of the verses just quoted, by saying, "And if you belong to Christ, then you are Abraham's offspring, heirs according to promise" (vs. 29). That is spiritual unity in belonging.

The crucial point is to decide whether the church is to redeem society as a social entity, or whether the church is to be an instrument for the redemption of men and women who will influence society. If the church is set up to establish a pattern for social justice, then the church must be the pacesetter and form herself into a heterogeneous unit where there is neither language, caste, or economic difference. However, this misapplies the teaching concerning the kingdom of God. Christ Himself recognized differences in society and among peoples.

He never predicted a human utopia even if making all alike would establish it. Nor did Christ ever imply that all men should be alike. All are of equal worth, not alike.

It would seem rather that recognition of differences and mutual respect for others as individuals within diversity of life-pattern would do more to influence society than to demand that all local churches be made up of unlike peoples just to try to present to the world a picture of unity. Diversity in harmony is more beautiful than amalgamation.

In no area do anthropology and theology come closer together than in this question. The homogeneous unit is an anthropological and sociological phenomenon. The church is theological. In the matter of evangelism, church planting, and church growth the sciences go hand in hand. True theology does not negate true anthropology. Neither does true anthropology interfere with true theology. The designer of the world and creator of man is the same One who revealed His eternal theological truth and plan of redemption to man. The two disciplines must always interact the one with the other. Anthropology must demand that theology does not speak beyond the intent of the revelation in reference to man where he is, and theology must demand that anthropology always recognize the authority under which it must operate, lest it become a law unto itself.

Another important consideration of the homogeneous–unit principle is to recognize that God prepares certain peoples at specific times to respond to the working of His Spirit among them. As coworker together with God (I Cor. 3:9, 2 Cor. 6:1), the evangelist is to recognize himself as an instrument of God in dealing with peoples in a special way, and be prepared to be God's minister among that people at that point in history.

All peoples are in process of change. All move along the continuum presented in chapter 9. Some are in explosion crises, others are in stagnation. Some are ready for dynamic response, others are hardened and apparently immobile. Where stagnation is in control, one may not expect homogeneous–unit response. An evangelist working in such a situation may see some individual response, with individuals moving in spite of the group, but can normally anticipate only slow and limited growth to occur. Personal discipleship would be the indicated pattern of evangelism.

Some are led of God to this ministry, and labor as coworkers and seed sowers, who must seek the grace of God to sustain them as they remain faithful to the call and appointment of God. Such laborers will pray constantly as intercessors for an outpouring of the Spirit of God upon the people, and the Lord may respond in His time to cause the group to come to life.

Others will be led of the Spirit to enter into more ripened fields, where God has prepared the field through many circumstances and historical events. There the workers will discover that God has already prepared a harvest, and move with God as coworkers in that harvest field. That may not always be recognized by observable phenomena and predictable by sociological criteria, and one must be sensitive to God's leading. But history does demonstrate that at certain times doors are open, and it can be seen that God is working among a distinct people in a very peculiar way. By His own will God moves the course of history of nations, and peoples. He did it with Israel. He did it with Babylon. He did it with Assyria. He did it with Nineveh. He did it with Germany. He did it with England. He did it with the Karens of Burma. He did it with the Bataks of Indonesia. He did it with the Nagas of Northeast India. He did it in Korea. He did it with the Ibos of Nigeria.

God, in His time and in His way, moves world history to prepare selected peoples at distinct times and places to respond to the call of His Holy Spirit, singling out particular groups by His special particularism among whom He works in special grace. History has shown that God's movement is ever on behalf of certain specific groups at particular times. Today some doors are open. Tomorrow other doors will be opened. Some of the open doors today will be closed tomorrow. Some of the closed doors today will be opened tomorrow. To move with the Spirit of God would normally mean to enter the open doors while they are open with special concentration of workers.

This does not mean neglect of any peoples. It demands mature sensitivity to the leading of the Spirit of God to work with Him where He is working. Some will be forerunners, and seed sowers, who understand their mission to be seed sowing, anticipating a harvest in its time. Others will be the reapers, gathering the fruit when it is ripe. Both labor in the fields, guided by the Holy Spirit who gives the increase, according to the times and seasons.

Recognition of the state of the people with whom one works will determine greatly the strategy one employs. Thus an understanding of both the nature of homogeneous-unit evangelism and the nature of the specific homogeneous unit with whom one is working will give guidance for the course of action to be followed and results to be anticipated. The recognition of the movement of the Spirit of God, resting upon whom He will rest and passing over whom He chooses to pass over, will always be a factor in the mind of the servant.

Some peoples are especially chosen and prepared, and some seem to be passed by. This is part of God's sovereignty, and can only be left to Him. Prayer alone is the only resource open to the human servant. This we are called upon to do.

Misunderstanding the issue can cause untold frustration and burden that is too heavy to bear. The individual may finally either collapse or give up under the strain. Understanding of the issue can give one assurance as he presses on, recognizing his position as colaborer in the fields, that some day may become "white unto harvest."

Bibliography

Kraft, Charles H. *Christianity in Culture*. Maryknoll, N.Y: Orbis Books, 1979.
_____and Wisley, Tom N., eds. *Readings in Dynamic Indigeneity*. Pasadena, CA: William Carey Library Publishers, 1979.
Liao, David C. E. *The Unresponsive: Resistant or Neglected?* Pasadena, CA: William Carey Library Publishers, 1979.
McGavran, Donald A. ed. *Church Growth and Christian Mission*. Pasadena, CA: William Carey Library Publishers, 1976.
_____*Understanding Church Growth*. Rev. ed. Grand Rapids: Eerdmans, 1980.

McQuilkin, J. Robertson. *Measuring the Church Growth Movement*. Rev. ed. Chicago: Moody Press, 1974.

Pentecost, Edward C. *Reaching the Unreached*. Pasadena, CA: William Carey Library Publishers, 1974.

Pickett, J.W., et al. *Church Growth and Group Conversion*. Pasadena, CA: William Carey Library Publishers, 1973.

Shearer, Roy E. *Wildfire: Church Growth in Korea*. Grand Rapids: Eerdmans, 1966.

Swank, Gerald O. *Frontier Peoples of Central Nigeria*. Pasadena, CA: William Carey Library Publishers, 1977.

Tippett, Alan R. *Church Growth and the Word of God*. Grand Rapids: Eerdmans, 1970.

_____ ed. *God, Man, and Church Growth*. Grand Rapids: Eerdmans, 1973.

_____ *Verdict Theology in Missionary Theory*. Pasadena, CA: William Carey Library Publishers, 1973.

Werning, Waldo J. *Vision and Strategy for Church Growth*. Chicago: Moody Press, 1977.

13

The Dynamics of Church Growth

Ever since our Lord commanded His disciples to "go into all the world and preach the gospel to all creation" Mark 16:15), His followers have sought to discover the best way to fulfill the command. They have tied together this last command with the word spoken to Peter, "Upon this rock I will build My church; and the gates of Hades shall not overpower it" (Matt. 16:18).

Believers have understood that Christ anticipated the planting of the church in every region and village, and among every people of the world.

The initial demonstration of fulfillment of the task came at Jerusalem on the day of Pentecost when people from almost every known language heard the preaching of Peter, and were convicted in their hearts by the Holy Spirit and believed. Upon returning to their own towns and peoples these believers became the first witnesses wherever they went.

The second wave of witnesses was the movement of the disciples who left Jerusalem because of the persecution while the apostles remained in the city (Acts 8:1).

Along with these two dynamic movements, Scripture presents individuals who became dynamic witnesses such as Stephen, the first martyr (Acts 7), and Philip, the evangelist (Acts 8). God was manifesting at the initiation of the church that two entities worked together to fulfill His purpose: *The*

Holy Spirit and men. Here is the first observation of the dynamics of church growth: *God at work through men of His choice.*

The Book of Acts follows with two distinct lines—outreach to the Jews, and outreach to the nations. The Jews had, throughout their history, the hope of the coming Messiah, but when He came they did not recognize Him. Yet, in spite of their rejection, God's new message still included them. Paul, with his evangelistic team, went out first to the synagogue in almost every place, but when cast out of the synagogue turned to those who would receive, and planted a church in every city to which the Holy Spirit directed. Here is a second observation of church growth: *Men, following the leading of the Holy Spirit, were effective church planters.* These were men, full of the Holy Spirit and of power, who spoke with authority.

For the initiation of missionary work as such, we turn to Acts 13 where the Holy Spirit moved with and through the church at Antioch to send out the first missionary team. Here it may be said is the third observation concerning church growth: *Approved messengers sent from the home (local) church.* Being called by the Holy Spirit and sent by the local church, they went with the recognition and endorsement of that body. They carried an identity. In Antioch that ministry was committed to a team of individuals who would share in the work together.

No one can doubt the movement of the Holy Spirit leading the first missionaries from place to place, even though the record shows how entirely human the factors were that moved the team on. Yet God was superintending the movements even though hidden from view at times. But Acts 16 clearly portrays how definitely the Holy Spirit had full control.

Moving through the course of church history one is reminded of the fact that in subsequent decades the church expanded greatly. In some areas it was accepted gladly. In some areas it was rejected entirely, and we discover a fourth observation: *Political, social, and religious factors influence the growth of the church in new areas.*

Kenneth Scott Latourette is the historian who most clearly analyzes the political, social, and religious influences on the spread of the gospel. In his seven-volume set, *A History Of the Expansion of Christianity*, Latourette delineates seven major questions by which he examines the spread of Christianity. These are:

1. What was the Christianity which spread?

That the Christianity that underwent expansion throughout history was not uniform from period to period nor from even one place to another during a given time span is posited. In one place there was Nestorianism, in another Roman Catholicism with its diverse groups, and in another Protestantism. Such diversity poses the question, Why?

2. Why did Christianity spread?

In seeking the answer to this question Latourette investigates the soil, the quality of the seed, the method of planting and cultivation and the combination of these factors that led to the spread of Christianity and to the influence on the local characteristics attributed to it.

3. Why has Christianity suffered reverses and at times met only partial successes?

Why did it fall before Islam in so much of the Mediterranean basin and in western and central Asia, and, more recently, in Russia before communism?

Why did Nestorianism meet with such little success in China? Why in the twentieth century, after being continuously present in India and China for a longer time than it took to win the majority of the population of the Roman Empire, does Christianity still enroll numerically a very small proportion of the peoples of either land?

(Note: Latourette does not judge between one form of Christianity and another. As a historian he considers any group that calls itself by the name *Christian* as equally valid. He makes no pronouncement concerning doctrine or creedal profession.)

4. By what processes did Christianity spread?

Latourette relates this question to question number 2 and seeks its answer in a study of missionary operations. He considers the accounts of the origin, development, and operations of the various orders, congregations, societies, committees, and boards which have actively undertaken the task of propagation, the methods employed, opposition encountered, and the results that have ensued.

5. What effect has Christianity had upon its environment?

Speculation and supposition play some role in dealing with this question. Absolute answers are not available, only observations. The same is true of the following question.

6. What was the effect of the environment on Christianity?

For example: What was the influence of Judaism on Christianity? What was the influence of Greek philosophy and thought pattern on the Roman Catholicism and on Greek Orthodoxy? Also how has Greek thought pattern influenced the Christianity of the West?

7. What bearing do the processes by which Christianity spread have upon the effect of Christianity on its environment, and of the environment upon Christianity?

For example: How much influence did the method used in penetrating Europe have on the characteristics of Christianity in Europe? In Latin America? In Africa?[1]

Latourette, a true historian, records the facts as he has been able to gather them. He is a recorder with insight and one who has been faithful to the task to which he set himself. One would like to find more answers in reading Latourette than he does find. One would hope to find a pattern that would emerge. But the student is left without the dynamics he would like to

1. Kenneth Scott Latourette, *A History of the Expansion of Christianity*, vol. 1, (Grand Rapids: Zondervan, 1970), pp. x-xv.

discover. He finds influences and relationships between various political, social, and religious elements, but he is left without any prophetic utterance that says, "Do this and thou shalt find success." No clear pattern of church planting emerges from the meticulous study. One is made very aware of the complexities, but no guiding star gives any great light. There are so many variables interacting that the prediction of outcome is impossible.

The great value of the study is not in any positive guidance regarding any pattern, but rather that the missionary must be aware of the multiplicity of operations and complexity of conflicting interests. Planting the church is a humanly complex undertaking, demanding a spiritual power above any human effort to accomplish the task.

This does not mean that one does not take into account every human factor to the greatest extent possible. Awareness of diversity and complexity makes one more malleable to the given situation that faces him. It makes him more dependent upon the Lord, and sensitive to His leading in every circumstance.

One major contribution that is gained from Latourette is the observation that *diversity of operation is vital to success.* God is not One to be bound to a formula. He did not create any two things alike. All of God's creation demonstrates His uniqueness in everything.

In reviewing history, biography, and case studies, we find diversity of elements in all. No two cases are alike. No pattern emerges to give a sure model to follow. Dependence on the Holy Spirit for each case is the only common denominator. What seemed to be applicable in one case may, or may not, be applicable in another. Likewise, elements of one may be applicable in another, but not the total.

In view of the history of the church one cannot avoid confrontation with certain questions. One is the expansion of the Roman Catholic Church. (At the time of the greatest outreach of the Roman Church the Protestant Church was sitting at home deliberating theological issues, trying to find itself and give expression to its position.) The Roman Church succeeded in its outreach by joining itself with colonizers, and by the formation of orders and societies that accepted responsibility and committed themselves to an arduous task. In this we observe three vital elements of expansion: 1) A goal; 2) Orderliness—or organization to accomplish the goal; 3) Personal commitment to that goal.

The fact that one may or may not agree with doctrinal positions disseminated does not detract from the dynamic of the expansion and the reality of church growth which may be presented as the following observation: *Establishing a goal, orderly planning to attain that goal, and personal commitment to that end are vital factors to effective church planting.*

History demonstrates that when Protestant missionary work began it was with the church sending missionaries, providing funds for the church buildings, supporting paid pastors and workers, and building institutions. Thus, in essence, the new church body was totally dependent upon the mother church or the mission society.

In the 1880s, John L. Nevius, a missionary to China and then Korea with the Presbyterian Church, proposed a new way. He demonstrated that the church could grow and expand through the spontaneous work of the ordinary church member, and that did not depend on a paid clergy. He taught 1) regular Bible study among the believers, 2) times of outreach visitation, and 3) simplicity of structure. He insisted that the new believers themselves build their own buildings with natural local material, and that no outside assistance was to be given. Thus the believers themselves became involved in every phase of development, giving themselves to it and sharing in it. Through their working and studying together Nevius built a community spirit among the followers of the Lord that radiated a living witness.

Perhaps a more well known individual is Roland Allen. Though not the initiator of the indigenous church principle, Allen became the popularizer of the concept.[2]

The dynamic that moved Allen was his conviction as stated.

2. For historical development of the theme, one should go to Henry Venn and Rufus Anderson, who formulated and debated the issues before Allen.

Many years ago my experience in China taught me that if our object was to establish in that country a church which might spread over the six provinces which then formed the diocese of North China, that object could only be attained if the first Christians who were converted by our labours understood clearly that they could by themselves, without any further assistance from us, not only convert their neighbours, but establish churches. That meant that the very first groups of converts must be so fully equipped with all spiritual authority that they could multiply themselves without any *necessary* reference to us: that, though, while we were there, they might regard us as helpful advisers, yet our removal should not at all mutilate the completeness of the church, or deprive it of anything necessary for its unlimited expansion. Only in such a way did it seem to me to be possible for churches to grow rapidly and securely over wide areas; for I saw that a single foreign bishop could not establish the church throughout the six provinces, over which he was nominally set, by founding mission stations governed by superintending missionaries, even if he had an unlimited supply of men and money at his command. The restraint of ordination to a few natives specially trained by us, and dependent for their own maintenance and the maintenance of their families upon salaries provided either by us or by the small native Christian community, and the absolute denial of any native episcopate at the beginning, seemed to me to render any wide expansion of the church impossible, and to suggest at the very beginning that there was something essentially foreign about the church which demanded the direction of a foreign governor.[3]

Being a missionary of the Society for the Propagation of the Gospel, an Anglican missionary society, Allen was a priest of the High Church of England, instructed in the Catholic understanding of church and priesthood. Therefore his proclamation takes on even more serious tones when one recognizes the degree of departure this spontaneous expansion concept was for him, his society, and missionaries of his day, the 1920s.

When Allen proposed a church that would be "self-sup-

---

3. Roland Allen, *The Spontaneous Expansion of the Church*, (Grand Rapids: Eerdmans, 1962), p. 1.

porting, self-governing, self-propagating" he was so far ahead of his time that his voice was hardly heard. It was not until the 1950s that his concept began to be adopted and the theme "To plant an indigeneous church" became the pattern.

Allen's dynamic principle for church growth centered in the term *spontaneous expansion*. He expressed it:

> This then is what I mean by spontaneous expansion. I mean the expansion which follows the unexhorted and unorganized activity of individual members of the Church explaining to others the Gospel which they have found for themselves; I mean the expansion which follows the irresistible attraction of the Christian Church for men who see its ordered life, and are drawn to it by desire to discover the secret of a life which they instinctively desire to share; I mean also the expansion of the Church by the addition of new churches.
>
> I know not how it may appear to others, but to me this unexhorted, unorganized, spontaneous expansion has a charm far beyond that of our modern highly organized missions. . . .[4]

Allen tied his position to the work of Paul who was his example. He stated in his preface of the second edition of his book *Missionary Methods: St. Paul's or Ours?:*

> St. Paul's churches were indigenous churches in the proper sense of the word; and I believe that the secret of their foundation lay in his recognition of the church as a local church (as opposed to our 'national churches') and in his profound belief and trust in the Holy Spirit indwelling his converts and the churches of which they were members, which enabled him to establish them at once with full authority. . . .[5]

The principle which Allen proposes may be stated: *New believers, filled by the Holy Spirit, are capable of conducting self-supporting, self-governing, and self-propagating churches.* However, experience has shown, that whereas the principle may

4. Ibid., p. 7.
5. Roland Allen, *Missionary Methods: St. Paul's or Ours?* 2d. ed. (Grand Rapids: Eerdmans, 1962), p. vii.

be ideally true, realistic teaching and instruction are vital to the new groups. The commission "teaching them to observe all that I commanded you" (Matt. 28:20) cannot be overlooked. Nor can the instruction of Paul to Timothy: "You therefore, my son, be strong in the grace that is in Christ Jesus. And the things which you have heard from me in the presence of many witnesses, these entrust to faithful men, who will be able to teach others also" (2 Tim. 2:1-2).

Scripturally a vital part of church planting and church growth is the nurturing experience. This does not come by initial evangelization that then abandons the new body of believers. Nor did Allen intend that. He meant that a new body had within itself the *potential* of becoming a mature body, and should be viewed as that, and not so structured that it would always be dependent upon foreign priests and control. He recognized that both a time element and an instructional pattern would be necessary. Yet he wanted, through the instruction, to plant the seed of self-dependence on the Spirit and not structure foreign control into the formation and development of the church. He did not nullify the necessity nor the effectiveness of teaching in order to bring new believers to maturity.

J. H. Bavinck in his *Introduction to the Science of Missions* gives a good balance to Allen and Nevius. He agrees that the practical work in the given local situation can best be carried on by national workers, but he insists that this does not mean abandonment of the new field. The church or body that initiated the work among a group of people still carries the responsibility for careful training of ministers. He says:

> But the heart of the matter is still the careful training of ministers. It is desirable that courses be conducted in the native language. The entire instruction must be directed to the world in which ministers will presently work. It must be biblical, completely biblical: they must learn to read the Bible attentively; they must learn to note calmly what God has to say concretely to them and to their people, in each part of the Bible. It is, therefore, also important to give careful instruction in the spiritual movements which surround their own people.

Their "old religions" must be studied, but new movements must also be contemplated and tested. Doctrinal instruction has as its special task the construction of a life and world view completely based on the Scriptures, a world view which consciously opposes everything which is not of God.

Finally there is the simple task of offering encouragement of building up the faith, and of strengthening the discouraged. There was a time when it was thought that young churches did not need this direct help and that they would rather be without it, but it is more and more evident that there is a very strong need for such aid and that they themselves openly acknowledge it. Within the young churches there is indeed a very great readiness to help, a great degree of self-denial, and of sacrifice, but discouragement easily arises, their power is weakened, and the fear enters their hearts that their labor is in vain. It is of great importance that missions do not withdraw too quickly, but that they stand ready to help bear this tremendous burden. Under the influence of Western culture, many countries in which missions are active are now threatened by materialism, agnosticism, and skepticism with respect to all religious values. Young Christians must also meet the challenge. Their old world had assigned a wide place to supernatural phenomena and magical forces. . . .[6]

From this balance we recognize that the church is an organism that requires interdependence, and within the body there are functions for which interrelationships were designed by the Lord in order that all might grow, "until we all attain to the unity of the faith, and of the knowledge of the Son of God, to a mature man, to the measure of the stature which belongs to the fulness of Christ" (Eph. 4:13). Thus the observation of church growth that emerges is: *The dynamic interdependence of the sending and receiving bodies on each other through the process of mutual maturing is a vital entity.*

Concurrent with Allen was Alexander Rattray Hay, founder of the New Testament Missionary Union of Latin America, who approached the question of the dynamics of church growth

6. J. H. Bavinck, *Introduction to the Science of Missions,* (Grand Rapids: Baker Book House, 1977), pp. 215-216.

from a strictly Biblical approach. He took the Book of Acts as a *pattern* that should be followed in every place. He wrote in the preface of his work, entitled: *The New Testament Order for Church and Missionary*,

> The matter is of such importance and the Scriptural pattern has been so obscured by centuries of ecclesiasticism that we have found it necessary to deal throughly with the Scriptural evidence and its significance. Reference is made also to the historical evidence, which so fully supports the teaching of Scripture.
>
> We do not offer this study as a text-book but simply as a statement of the experiences and guidance which the Lord has given. The only authoritative and complete text-book on church order and missionary procedure is God's Word. Our desire is to point to that Word.[7]

Hay had experienced twenty-five years of apparently fruitless ministry in Argentina, following the pattern of most missions of his day. In frustration he turned to study the work of the New Testament evangelists to try to find a pattern that would be applicable. He reports that he found it in the New Testament principles. They present themselves in three aspects: 1) By example, as Christ and the apostles are studied; 2) By instruction, as the structure of the church is understood, being revealed in Scripture; and 3) By application, in which he propounds the passing on of the New Testament order for the church to the newly formed body of believers.

Hay proposed:

1. That the evangelists should be prepared instruments.
2. That Christ goes with them.
3. That the evangelistic team was "international but not foreign."
4. That recruits to spread the church be from the "new" church, not more foreign missionaries sent in.

7. Alexander Rattray Hay, *The New Testament Order for Church and Missionary*, (Temperley, Argentina: New Testament Missionary Union, 1947), p. 8.

5. That "new" churches be taught to support the evangelists, and that evangelists live on the provision of the churches they founded.

With regard to the church organization, Hay declared:

A careful and unbiased study of the New Testament will make it abundantly clear that a full and detailed revelation is given regarding the structure of the Church and that all the congregations planted in Apostolic times were organized in accordance with that pattern.[8]

A review of the years of ministry that followed shows that those congregations formed after this procedure was implemented remained as rather small bodies of closely knit units that were intent upon transferring the New Testament church into their life and times. The problem was that the New Testament pattern was understood to be Biblical but it never became relevant.

Hay proposed some wonderful thoughts concerning the church in its outreach and structure, but failed to bring it to living reality. The life-giving dynamic was lost in the process. It became a pattern to follow; a mold for new bodies to conform to. But it never became a living, self-propagating organism.

By this we observe that *one dynamic of church growth is the necessity of that body to relate its own identity to its own context.* Function is vital and equal in all environments, but form and structure are relevant to people where they are and where they live.

Hay and Allen were both grappling with essentially the same problem. Institutionalized propagation had failed. They were both seeking answers. Allen proposed the indigenous aspect. Hay proposed a Biblical pattern answer. Allen lost some of the Biblical absolutes that were necessary. Hay lost some of the human relevance to meet the needs of the changing social, cultural, political needs. Hay demonstrates that a

8. Ibid., p. 127.

pattern answer is insufficient. Allen demonstrates that a Biblical absolute must lay the foundation. We learn from both.

More recently, about 1955, the Missionary Studies Department of the International Missionary Council and the World Council of Churches undertook a series of in-depth studies to determine what factors influenced individuals and local churches in different places. Their studies were to follow somewhat the seven steps of Latourette as guide for research of individual groups or churches. Their thinking reflected his pattern. John V. Taylor, a sociologist and missionary of the Church Missionary Society of London, undertook an analysis of the growth of the church in Buganda, Africa, and has made his findings available in a report with that title.

In his discussion of the question of "Response and Responsibility," Taylor writes:

> The fact is that this thing that was taking place, the church dormant waking into response and becoming the church militant, was happening at a deeper and more subtle level than most missionaries were aware of. The Spirit was blowing where it listed, bringing into its mysterious operation many factors which are often omitted from the categories of our theology.
>
> The process by which, in this situation, people were becoming Christians, and that by which the new church was becoming more holy and more effective, seem to have been one and continuous. By analysis it can be seen to consist of four consecutive components which we might call, Congruence, Detachment, Demand, and Crisis.[9]

By *congruence* Taylor meant, "the fitting together, of the new community and the new ideas, with the old structure and the emergent aspirations which already existed."[10]

By *detachment* Taylor meant, "the loosening of the ties which bound men to the old way and the old pattern, gradually

9. John V. Taylor, *The Growth of the Church in Buganda: An Attempt at Understanding,* (1958; reprint ed., Westport, CT: Greenwood Press, 1979), p. 43.
10. Ibid.

bringing them to an independence sufficient to set them free to make the choices which the gospel was demanding."[11] This implied revolutionary thought into the minds of the people.

By *demand* Taylor meant, "the demand which people felt the gospel laid upon them. This was something inherent in the gospel itself, which appealed directly to the conscience and to which the conscience gave assent."[12]

Among the demands noted were separation from worship and offerings to their idols, and equality of all believers together in the church. Here the chief and the servant met on common ground.

By *crisis* Taylor explains:

> Gradually individuals and groups have found themselves beginning to belong to the new thing; almost unnoticed they have been eased away from their homogeneity with the old, and have grown independent; steadily their conscience has been made aware of something demanding some specific change of attitude or behavior. But none can tell how real a response, or how permanent a transfer has been made, until suddenly some development precipitates a crisis, for a moment the old and the new ways fly apart and people are either found adhering to the new, or they spring back to the old. This very clarification itself introduces a new situation, a fresh chapter as it were. Then the moment of revelation passes and the continuing process starts up again out of sight.[13]

Taylor concluded that his findings might at least be representative of patterns experienced elsewhere. His observations give us cause to consider the four elements of church planting among potential target groups: *Formation of a new group, separating themselves from the old, because the demands inherent in the gospel require separation, proven by the crisis that solidifies the group into a new body.*

Much more recently, Dr. Donald McGavran has proposed

11. Ibid., p. 44.
12. Ibid., p. 45.
13. Ibid., p. 49.

a strong and very well supported emphasis on the "homogeneous-unit" approach as basic to church growth. He believes God wants His church to exist among every people and tongue, tribe, and nation. Being a disciple of J. Wascomb Pickett in the country of India, and seeing the homogeneous-unit approach in action, McGavran proceeded to study the phenomenon more deeply and more widely. He expanded his research to other countries and compared the results of those who labored on a one-by-one principle with those who operated within group action. The results of his investigation convinced McGavran that the homogeneous-unit principle was the way to move to see the church of Jesus Christ established among every people. He concluded that not all groups would respond positively. If a group did not, it was in order to move on to another group among whom the Spirit of God was working, and whose hearts the Lord had prepared to receive the messenger and the message.

The fundamental concept proposed by McGavran is that people like to become followers of Christ and to operate within their own known framework, without having to give up culture and customs to do so. He proposes that people should not have to separate themselves from their normal patterns of life to take on a foreignness. He proposes that multi-individual conversion patterns are normative and are of the Spirit. Thus he has propounded very enthusiastically and convincingly the homogeneous-unit approach to church planting and his body of followers is growing larger every day.

Perhaps stated as McGavran's observation we could conclude: *The most effective way to see the church planted among "all nations" is through the homogeneous-unit approach.*

This approach certainly strengthens the arguments of Nevius and Allen in their indigenous principles and spontaneous growth patterns.

At the same time that McGavran was studying the homogeneous-unit approach, J. Edwin Orr was concentrating on the revival movements as initiators of churches and mission outreach. He has concluded that every revival resulted in new expansion and outreach. When people were renewed in their relationship to their Lord something happened and the spontaneous testimony of those awakened people spread to affect others. The witness at home expanded and concern for the lost elsewhere increased. Giving to missions increased, and commitment to missions and missionary volunteers increased.

Orr observes that out of the Great Awakenings, movements resulted and new works emerged. However, out of these movements we do not find any new "church growth" patterns established. There was presence, proclamation, service, and spontaneous witness from true heart concern. Wherever reawakened witnesses went, new churches were formed. The observable pattern was: *Spontaneous growth out of lay witness.*

Concurrent with McGavran and Orr, Dr. George W. Peters committed himself to an analysis of what he called Saturation Evangelism. Many mission bodies were organizing existing churches in a plan to Mobilize for Action. These programs were producing new and growing churches. Such movements as Evangelism in Depth in Latin America, New Life for All in Nigeria, and Mobilization Evangelism in Japan were making themselves known. All had the perspective of mobilizing believers of a given area to present mass action with lay involvement.

Peters, a theologian, concluded his studies, convinced that the issue of Saturation Evangelism was a theological concern as well as practical application. He states in his work entitled *Saturation Evangelism:*

> Mobilization of all believers in evangelizing is not only a serious and practical question; it is foremost a theological concern. Has God actually willed that every believer become an active evangelizing agent, or is it sufficient to be only a supporting evangelizing standby? Are there not many different gifts of the Spirit and assignments according to these gifts? Is it the design of God that every believer personally participate in the evangelizing process of the world? If so, what is his part? How is he to be involved?[14]

14. George W. Peters, *Saturation Evangelism,* (Grand Rapids: Zondervan, 1970), p. 31.

Peters gives the answer to his own question by stating:

The answers to these questions can be given by another question: Is every believer . . . a priest of God? Do we realistically and not only ideally and theoretically believe in the universal priesthood of all believers? It is time that we put some realism into our idealism.[15]

To Peters the spontaneous nature of the witness results in the dynamic movement in planting new churches. Thus spontaneous witness takes on various forms, in different cultures. No two will be exactly alike, but all will have the same dynamic. He proposes four distinctives of Saturation Evangelism:

1. *Saturation evangelism aims at gospel saturation of the community and country, and also of the believers and churches.* It presents the Gospel in spoken and written form to every people of the land, to every strata of society, to every home and individual. It is a serious attempt to saturate the land with the good news of God, overlooking no area and no community. It is an in-depth evangelism program literally attempting to fulfill the command of Christ to preach the Gospel to every creature. . . .[16]

2. *Saturation evangelism makes a strenuous attempt to reverse an age-old practice in evangelism, best described as church centripetalism, and transform it into dynamic, evangelistic centrifugalism.* Traditional evangelism has become structured as to time, place and personnel. Somehow the sentiment prevails among most church people that only at times of church-sponsored evangelistic programs are church members to be seriously concerned and engaged in doing a part in bringing people under the sound of the Gospel. Seemingly, only at times of evangelism programs in the church do Christians become involved in the evangelistic activities of the church and manifest their interest in bringing people to the church to be evangelized. Structured church evangelism holds the members captive as to time of evangelism. . . .[17]

15. Ibid.
16. Ibid., p. 39.
17. Ibid., p. 40.

3. *Saturation evangelism follows a predetermined and coordinated schedule of simultaneous activities throughout all cooperating churches.* This makes for unity of spirit and depth of impact. It begins with series of meetings for purposes of organization, orientation, and inspiration to set the overall stage for the thrust. Next comes the time of intensive instruction in retreats for pastors and leading laymen. These in turn carry these instructions into the local churches, where men and women are being mobilized and equipped for evangelism.

At the same time prayer groups are initiated and multiplied to undergird the movement and to become prayer evangelism cells. The records of the latter are perhaps the most encouraging and significant phenomenon in the history of the church at present. Thousands of such cells continue for years to follow. . . . [18]

4. *Saturation evangelism earnestly endeavors to enlist in the movement as many churches, missions, and denominations as will cooperate in an evangelical and evangelistic program in order to express the unity of the body of Christ.* This unity strengthens the cause of evangelism, involves and trains as many people as make themselves available, and creates the greatest possible impact upon the churches and communities. [19]

What then are we to determine concerning the dynamics of church growth as observed from the review of history, research, and grappling with the issues involved? From both Biblical and experience-oriented sources we must approach the question. The following emerges as a proposal:

1. God wants and intends His church to grow. That issue is not debated. God sent His Son to redeem lost men. Christ said, ". . . I will build My church; and the gates of Hades shall not overpower it" (Matt.16:18). Christ commanded His disciples to "go therefore and make disciples of all the nations" (Matt. 28:19). "Go into all the world and preach the gospel to all creation" (Mark 16:15).

2. God works through men of His choice to accomplish His purpose. These may be especially endowed, or chosen, or committed. But God's instruments are men.

18. Ibid., p. 41.
19. Ibid., p. 42.

3. God's men are filled with God's power by the Holy Spirit. God never calls one to be "coworker" to let him go to work alone. He is always with that one to "empower" him.

4. Men are sent out from local churches to spread what they have learned. God prepares His servants through a period of learning first, and experience, and this experience and learning is recognized by those who know him.

5. Biblical absolutes are determined by clear Biblical instruction, applicable in every culture and language. Political, social, cultural, and religious factors influence the local church in each region.

6. Diversity of operation is vital for success, governed by the control of the Holy Spirit in such a way as to be applicable to each given situation.

7. Church planting demands establishing a goal, orderly planning to attain that goal, and personal commitment to that goal.

8. New believers have the potential of becoming self-supporting, self-governing, and self-propagating local churches; but instruction in the Word cannot be sacrificed. Rather the dynamic interdependence of the whole body is essential for the growth and unity of all.

9. Function of the local church is Biblically comprehended and spiritually directed. Form and structure are culturally related and relevant to each people.

10. New believers are to be formed into a new group, separating themselves from the old religion with its attachments, that they may become "new creatures in Christ Jesus" because the demands inherent in the gospel require separation which will be proven by the crisis that solidifies the group into a new body.

11. The homogeneous–unit approach is the most effective and versatile way of seeing the church planted among all nations.

12. When God's people are awakened, they begin to move, to witness, to reach out, and others are affected and brought into new congregations of believers.

13. The mobilization of all believers in a spontaneous out-

reach is the culmination of theological truth put into the highest order of practice.

Bibliography

Allen, Roland. *Missionary Methods: St. Paul's or Ours?* Grand Rapids: Eerdmans, 1962.

————*The Spontaneous Expansion of the Church*. Grand Rapids: Eerdmans, 1962.

Bavinck, J. H. *An Introduction to the Science of Missions*. Grand Rapids: Baker Book House, 1977.

Hay, Alexander Rattray. *The New Testament Order for Church and Missionary*. Temperley, Argentina: The New Testament Missionary Union, 1947.

Kraft, Charles H. *Christianity in Culture*. Maryknoll, NY: Orbis Books, 1979.

Latourette, Kenneth Scott. *A History of the Expansion of Christianity*. Vol. 1. Grand Rapids: Zondervan, 1970.

McGavran, Donald A., ed. *Church Growth and Christian Missic.ı*. Pasadena, CA: William Carey Library Publishers, 1976.

————*Understanding Church Growth*. Rev. ed. Grand Rapids: Eerdmans, 1980.

McQuilkin, J. Robertson. *Measuring the Church Growth Movement*. Chicago: Moody Press, 1974.

Nevius, John L. *The Planting and Development of Missionary Churches*. Phillipsburg, NJ: Presbyterian and Reformed Publishing, 1974.

Orr, J. Edwin. *The Second Evangelical Awakening in Britain*. Wheaton, IL: Van Kampen Press, 1949.

Pentecost, Edward C. *Reaching the Unreached*. Pasadena, CA: William Carey Library Press, 1974.

Peters, George W. *Saturation Evangelism*. Grand Rapids: Zondervan, 1970.

Shearer, Roy E. *Wildfire: Church Growth in Korea*. Grand Rapids: Eerdmans, 1966.

Taylor, John V. *The Growth of the Church in Buganda: An Attempt at Understanding*. 1958. Revised. Westport, CT: Greenwood Press, 1979.

Tippett, Alan R. *Church Growth and the Word of God*. Grand Rapids: Eerdmans, 1970.

————ed. *God, Man, and Church Growth*. Grand Rapids: Eerdmans, 1973.

————*Verdict Theology in Missionary Theory*. Pasadena, CA: William Carey Library Publishers, 1973.

Werning, Waldo J. *Vision and Strategy for Church Growth*. Chicago: Moody Press, 1977.

Womack, David A. *Breaking the Stained-Glass Barrier*. New York: Harper and Row Publishers, 1973.

14

The Nature of
the Spiritual Warfare

God has an enemy who is determined to destroy both Him and His work. In the Garden of Eden he tried to utterly destroy man. When Christ came to earth he tried to utterly destroy Him. Even though God is the sovereign, eternal One, the Creator of all, He has allowed Satan to rise up, that He might demonstrate His love and grace to man, and His omnipotence and sovereignty over all. Satan, the deceiver, the destroyer, the subtle one, is a very real entity with which missions must deal, and which missionaries face as individuals.

The foregoing chapters have dealt largely with people in social and cultural relationships. We have seen how the social sciences apply to help the understanding of interpersonal communication of the gospel. The remaining aspect to be considered is in the spiritual realm, dealing with the intangible yet very real spiritual conflict. Without an understanding of the spiritual forces of darkness that are satanic, the mission enterprise is doomed to failure.

Missions face two opposing forces. The first is the fallen nature of man. As a son of Adam all human beings are by nature sinful creatures (Rom. 5:12-21). Both body and mind, as well as society and culture, have been affected by sin (Rom. 1:28). As a result missions must consider its confrontation with people who have become incapacitated to know and do that which is right in and of themselves. Cultural practices demonstrate a heart and mind that is deformed, turned away from that which is right, just, and honorable; many practices are guided by misdirected thoughts. Both individuals and society suffer. Missionaries face degenerate peoples, yet love them in spite of their thoughts and actions. An understanding of their condition helps one deal lovingly, patiently, and kindly. It gives a reason for behavior. Understanding the human condition helps one accept a person for what he is, while at the same time desiring to see him be what he can be as a regenerate individual. This aspect of the depravity of the human nature and its results is a subject of theology beyond the intent of this study, and will not be further pursued here, but an understanding of the fact is essential.

The second of the two opposing forces the missionary faces is the satanic powers. From the beginning Satan began his work of deception. Ever since, he has been following the same line. He is bent on deceiving men, trying to make them believe a lie and lose the redemption that God has offered.

Along with Satan are an unknown number of fallen angels, demons, powers, evil forces, that both influence and indwell humans. Scripture relates how people were "demon possessed" and subjected to their rule and domination. (See Mark 5.) Paul writes of "angels," "principalities," "powers," that would try to separate men from the love of God (Rom. 8:38). In writing to the Ephesians he writes of "the Prince of the power of the air" as being that "spirit that is now working in the sons of disobedience" (Eph. 2:2). Later he writes "For our struggle is not against flesh and blood, but against the rulers, against the powers, . . . against the spiritual forces of wickedness in the heavenly places" (Eph. 6:12).

Peter writes of the angels that sinned (2 Pet. 2:4). Jude alludes to spirits, demons, powers (Jude 6). Luke speaks of them as being intelligent creatures (Luke 8:28). Matthew shows them as cruel, causing human grief and pain (Matt. 12:22). They are shown to be totally evil and "unclean" (Matt. 10:1; Mark 1:27; 3:11, 4:36; Acts 8:7; Rev. 16:13).

Missionaries likewise give testimony to the reality of the

spirits and demons, telling of the fear of peoples who are afflicted with their presence and of experiences of confrontation personally.

Scriptures would seem to indicate that there are two categories of opposing forces. One is the opposition of personal, spiritual beings. The other is the influence of nonpersonal powers. The one would be the personal demonic forces that can at times be identified, such as seen in Ephesians, where the phenomenon of demon possession was well known (Acts 19:11-16). The other is simply powers or influences. Berkhof in *Christ and the Powers* states, "[These] Powers rule over human life outside of Christ."[1] He attributes the death of Christ to such powers, that dominated men to do their evil deed.

These influences may be observed in government agencies who seem to do all possible to oppose the gospel messenger by denying visa privileges, by denying right of assembly, by denying right of witness, or any other possible hindrance that might be imposed. They may or may not be influenced by demons or spirits, but the effect is powerful opposition to the gospel message and messenger. The missionary is not as much concerned over whether the powers are demons or fallen angels or world-influencing powers, as he is in recognizing that such influences do exist and that they are real.

These powers have become real entities with which unregenerate men come face to face in real-life situations. They are not the result of superstition or of pagan imaginations. They are entities which inhibit and separate man from the love of God. They are powers that demand submission from men. They are powers that demand offerings and worship. They are realities that have power to inflict sickness and strange behavior on their subjects. They are realities that influence life patterns. Many tribes are governed by taboos which, out of fear, control actions. Sacrifices and offerings of appeasement are offered to the spirits in order to bring peace.

1. Hendrikus Berkhof, *Christ and the Powers*, trans. John Howard Yoder (Scottdale, PA: Herald Press, 1962), p. 15.

Belief in devils, demons, and evil spirits is universal. Anthropologists as well as theologians are convinced of the reality of such other-world forces. The use of amulets and talismans, fetishes and objects of magic is universal. These are worn or carried to protect against evil because of fear of these entities.

The Ming people of central Nigeria offer their blood sacrifice of a goat each February, sprinkling the blood on the door of their hut, to keep away the evil spirits from the house. In West Africa the fetish is an object which is impregnated with a medicine and worn by an individual to keep away the evil spirits. The medicine man has acquaintance with the ways of the evil spirits and knows that medicine is required to ward off the given spirit that would be prone to attack.

Idowu in *African Traditional Religion* states that animism, where it appears in Africa, is ". . . belief in, recognition and acceptance of the fact of the existence of, spirits who may use material objects as temporary residences and manifest their presence and actions through natural objects and phenomena."[2]

With the reality of demons, evil spirits, and strange powers, the missionary is engaged in a spiritual warfare. He faces confrontation with the depraved, sinful nature of man, and the spiritual encounter of the powers of spiritual darkness.

Paul was aware of the conflict, and under the direction of the Holy Spirit, wrote accordingly:

> Finally, be strong in the Lord, and in the strength of His might. Put on the full armor of God, that you may be able to stand firm against the schemes of the devil. For our struggle is not against flesh and blood, but against the rulers, against the powers, against the world forces of this darkness, against the spiritual forces of wickedness in the heavenly places. Therefore take up the full armor of God, that you may be able to resist in the evil day, and having done everything, to stand firm (Eph. 6:10-13).

2. E. Bolaji Idowu, *African Traditional Religion* (Maryknoll, NY: Orbis Books, 1973), p. 173.

The weapons consist of the Word of God and prayer. There are only two. Here the most well developed methodology of evangelism is to no avail. The best techniques of communication amount to nothing. The best laid plans of evangelism and most basic church growth principles dissolve into utter fancy.

Missionary activity is finally a spiritual warfare. The enemy is not ultimately man, but Satan. The forces one encounters are not human, but otherworldly. They are the forces of darkness. The host of the anti-God powers work against the missionary, because they are working against God and His purpose. However, the Word of God is the offensive weapon given to the servant of the Lord, and prayer is his defense. By it mountains are moved, and protection is granted. Spiritual battles are fought and won in the prayer arena.

Paul went on in Ephesians 6 to give instructions to the believers concerning the manner in which the enemy is to be overcome:

> Stand firm therefore, having girded your loins with truth, and having put on the breastplate of righteousness, and having shod your feet with the preparation of the gospel of peace; in addition to all, taking up the shield of faith with which you will be able to extinguish all the flaming missiles of the evil one. And take the helmet of salvation, and the sword of the Spirit, which is the word of God. With all prayer and petition pray at all times in the Spirit, and with this in view, be on the alert with all perseverance and petition for all the saints (Eph. 6:14-18).

Example after example could be given of the effectiveness of prayer in the spiritual battlefield. Almost all of the biographies of missionaries recount the prayer life of those servants. No one enters into the spiritual battlefield of missionary service without considering the forces against which he is launching his attack, nor without learning how to use both the offensive and defensive weapons available to him. The missionary is attacking the strongholds of Satan. Satan has had years to raise his defenses and prepare his fortresses. His subjects are well trained in fighting off the advances of Christianity. Satan is well established behind his walled defense. How can the missionary penetrate those defenses? Surely not by his own might, power, imaginations, methodology, strategy, or any humanly devised means. If he penetrates it will be because the Holy Spirit of God, using the Word of God, moves into the enemy camp and gives the victory.

To Paul, prayer was an earnest striving of the soul; to Jacob it was a wrestling with God; to Christ it was with strong crying and tears. Prayer is an instrument by which God is moved to do wonders, and people are released from overcoming powers that would enslave them.

Satan will not let go of his subjects easily. It will take the command of God for Satan to release those he is holding captive. No man can command Satan to set his captives free. But prayer will move God to command him to do so.

Prayer for the preacher brings illumination of his messages. Prayer for the missionary brings release of captives from the powers of darkness. No wonder Paul writes: "Pray without ceasing" (1 Thess. 5:17).

Prayer is, finally, intercession. It is the fulfillment of Peter's statement: "But you are a chosen race, a royal priesthood . . ." (1 Pet. 2:9). The priest was one who stood before the nation on behalf of God, and before God on behalf of the people. He was an intercessor. So is the missionary. He is an intercessor between God and the people whom his heart longs to see become followers of Christ and members of His body. He knows the power of evil to deceive, and the power of darkness to blind. He knows that the only resource he has to liberate men rests in his laying hold of God on their behalf.

Prayer and the Word of God become the two final instruments in the missionary's grasp. He must make full use of them under the direction of the Holy Spirit. Herein lies his strength and his potential victory.

The promise of John stands: "Greater is He who is in you than he who is in the world" (1 John 4:4).

Bibliography

Barnhouse, Donald G. *The Invisible War*. Grand Rapids: Zondervan, 1965.

Berkhof, Hendrikus. *Christ and the Powers*. Translated from the Dutch by John Howard Yoder. Scottdale, PA: Herald Press, 1962.

Bounds, Edward McKendree. *Power Through Prayer*. Grand Rapids: Zondervan, 1964.

Caird, George Bradford. *Principalities and Powers: A Study in Pauline Theology*. Oxford: Clarendon Press, 1956.

DeHaan, Richard, and VanderLugt, Herbert. *Satan, Satanism, and Witchcraft*. Grand Rapids: Zondervan, 1972.

Demon Experiences in Many Lands. Chicago: Moody Press, 1960.

Idowu, E. Bolaji. *African Traditional Religion*. Maryknoll, NY: Orbis Books, 1973.

Kelly, Henry A. *The Devil, Demonology, and Witchcraft*. Garden City, NY: Doubleday, 1968.

Lindsey, Hal. *Satan is Alive and Well on Planet Earth*. New York: Bantam Books, 1974.

Nevius, John L. *Demon Possession*. Grand Rapids: Kregel Publications, 1973.

Pentecost. J. Dwight. *Your Adversary the Devil*. Grand Rapids: Zondervan, 1976.

Peterson, Robert. *Roaring Lion: Spiritism in Borneo Challenged by the Power of Christ*. London: Overseas Missionary Fellowship, 1968.

Philpott, Kent. *A Manual of Demonology and the Occult*. Grand Rapids: Zondervan, 1976.

Unger, Merrill F. *Biblical Demonology*. Wheaton, IL: Van Kampen Press, 1952.

_____*Demons in the World Today*. Wheaton, IL: Tyndale House, 1971.

White, Hugh W. *Demonism Verified and Analyzed*. New York: Gordon Press, n.d.

General Bibliography

Allen, Roland. *Missionary Methods: St. Paul's or Ours?* Grand Rapids: Eerdmans, 1962.

_____*The Spontaneous Expansion of the Church.* Grand Rapids: Eerdmans, 1962.

Anderson, Gerald H., ed. *The Theology of the Christian Mission.* New York: McGraw-Hill, 1961.

Arensberg, Conrad M., and Niehoff, Arthur H. *Introducing Social Change: A Manual for Community Development.* Chicago: Aldine Publishing, 1967.

Barnett, Homer G. *Innovations: The Basis of Cultural Change.* New York: McGraw-Hill, 1963.

Barnhouse, Donald G. *The Invisible War.* Grand Rapids: Zondervan, 1965.

Bascom, W. R., and Herskovits, M. J., eds. *Continuity and Change in African Cultures.* Chicago: University of Chicago Press, 1958.

Bavinck, J. H. *An Introduction to the Science of Missions.* Grand Rapids: Baker Book House, 1977.

Beaver, Robert Pierce, ed. *The Gospel and Frontier Peoples.* Pasadena, CA: William Carey Library Publishers, 1973.

Belew, M. Wendell, *Missions in the Mosaic.* Atlanta: Southern Baptist Convention, 1974.

Benedict, Ruth. *Patterns of Culture.* Boston: Houghton Mifflin, 1961.

Berkhof, Hendrikus. *Christ and the Powers.* Translated from the Dutch by John Howard Yoder. Scottdale, PA: Herald Press, 1962.

Blauw, Johannes. *The Missionary Nature of the Church: A Survey of the Biblical Theology of Missions.* New York: McGraw-Hill, 1952.

Bounds, Edward McKendree. *Power Through Prayer.* Grand Rapids: Zondervan, 1953.

Budge, E. A. Wallis. *Amulets and Talismans.* New York: Macmillan Co., Collier Books, 1970.

Caird, George Bradford. *Principalities and Powers: A Study in Pauline Theology*. Oxford: Clarendon Press, 1956.

Carver, William Owen. *Missions in the Plan of the Ages*. Old Tappan, NJ: Fleming H. Revell, 1909.

Chafer, Lewis Sperry. *Systematic Theology*, vol. 4. Grand Rapids: Zondervan, 1947.

Coleman, Richard J. *Issues of Theological Conflict*. Rev. ed. Grand Rapids: Eerdmans, 1980.

Coleman, Robert E. *The Master Plan of Evangelism*. Old Tappan, NJ: Fleming H. Revell, 1978.

Conn, Harvie M. *Theological Perspectives on Church Growth*. Phillipsburg, NJ: Presbyterian and Reformed Publishing, 1976.

Costas, Orlando E. *The Church and its Mission: A Shattering Critique from the Third World*. Wheaton: IL: Tyndale House, 1975.

Dale, Kenneth J. *Circle of Harmony: A Case Study in Popular Japanese Buddhism with Implications for Christian Mission*. Pasadena, CA: William Carey Library Publishers, 1975.

Dayton, Edward R., and Fraser, David A. *Planning Strategies for World Evangelization*. Grand Rapids: Eerdmans, 1980.

DeHaan, Richard, and Vanderlugt, Herbert. *Satan, Satanism, and Witchcraft*. Grand Rapids: Zondervan, 1972.

Dennet, Herbert. *Christian Communications in a Changing World*. London: Victor Press, 1968.

Devlali Findings. *Report of the Findings Committee and Working Groups of the India Congress on Mission and Evangelism, January 12-19, 1977*. New Delhi, India: Kalpana Printing House, 1977.

Edersheim, Alfred. *Life and Times of Jesus the Messiah*. 2 vol. Grand Rapids: Eerdmans, 1972.

Getz, Gene A. *The Measure of a Church*. Ventura, CA: Regal Books, 1975.
――――*Sharpening the Focus of the Church*. Chicago: Moody Press, 1976.

Glover, Robert Hall. *The Biblical Basis of Missions*. Chicago: Moody Press, 1966.

Gluckman, Max. *Custom and Conflict in Africa*. New York: Barnes and Noble, 1969.

Greenway, Roger S. *A World to Win: Preaching World Missions Today*. Grand Rapids: Baker Book House, 1975.

Grunlan, Stephen A., and Mayers, Marvin K. *Cultural Anthropology: A Christian Perspective*. Grand Rapids: Zondervan, 1979.

Gulick, Sidney Lewis. *The East and the West: A Study of Their Psychic and Cultural Characteristics*. Rutland, VT: Charles E. Tuttle, 1963.

Guthrie, Donald. *New Testament Introduction*. Rev. ed. Downers Grove, IL: Inter-Varsity Press, 1971.

Hahn, Ferdinand. *Missions in the New Testament*. Translated by Frank Clarke. Geneva, AL: Alec R. Allenson, 1965.

Hall, Edward T. *The Silent Language.* 1973. Reprint. Westport, CT: Greenwood Publishing, 1980.

Hanson, James H. *What is the Church? Its Nature and Function.* Minneapolis: Augsburg Publishing, 1961.

Hay, Alexander Rattray. *The New Testament Order for Church and Missionary.* Temperley, Argentina: New Testament Missionary Union, 1947.

Herskovits, Melville J. *Acculturation: The Study of Culture Contact.* Magnolia, MA: Peter Smith Publishers, 1958.

_____*Cultural Dynamics.* New York: Alfred A. Knopf, 1964.

Hesselgrave, David J. *Communicating Christ Cross-Culturally.* Grand Rapids: Zondervan, 1978.

_____ed. *New Horizons in World Mission.* Grand Rapids: Baker Book House, 1980.

_____*Planting Churches Cross-Culturally.* Grand Rapids: Baker Book House, 1980.

_____ed. *Theology and Mission.* Grand Rapids: Baker Book House, 1978.

Horner, Norman A., ed. *Protestant Crosscurrents in Mission.* Nashville: Abingdon Press, 1968.

Idowu, E. Bolaji. *African Traditional Religion.* Maryknoll, NY: Orbis Books, 1973.

Jackson, B. F. J., ed. *Communication: Learning for Churchmen.* Nashville: Abingdon Press, 1968.

Jansen, John Frederick. *Exercises in Interpreting Scripture.* Philadelphia: Geneva Press, 1968.

Johnston, Arthur. *The Battle for World Evangelism.* Wheaton: Tyndale House, 1978.

_____*World Evangelism and the Word of God.* Minneapolis: Bethany Fellowship, 1974.

Kane, J. Herbert. *Christian Missions in Biblical Perspective.* Grand Rapids: Baker Book House, 1976.

_____*Understanding Christian Missions.* Grand Rapids: Baker Book House, 1978.